THE OFFICE PARTY

THE OFFICE PARTY

by John Godber

JOSEF WEINBERGER PLAYS

LONDON

THE OFFICE PARTY
First published in 1995
by Josef Weinberger Ltd (pka Warner Chappell Plays Ltd)
12-14 Mortimer Street
London W1T 3JJ
www.josef-weinberger.com / plays@jwmail.co.uk

The author asserts his moral right to be identified as the author of the work.

ISBN 978 0 85676 168 3

THE OFFICE PARTY was first presented at the Palace Theatre, Watford on 11th November, 1994, with the following cast:

GAVIN	Michael Simpkins
ANDY	Iain Rogerson
BOB	Bill Ilkley
PIPPA	Gaynor Faye
PATTY	Gill Tompkins
LEE	Dan Swinton
JO	Mandana Jones

Directed by Richard Lewis
Designed by Robert Jones

An earlier version of THE OFFICE PARTY was presented by Nottingham Playhouse in association with Hull Truck Productions at Nottingham Playhouse in September 1992, with the following cast:

GAVIN	Gareth Tudor Price
ANDY	Mark Addy
BOB	Steven Alvey
PIPPA	Gaynor Faye
PATTY	Meriel Scholfield
LEE	Nicholas Lane
JO	Rebecca Clay

Directed by John Godber
Designed by Robert Jones

CAST OF CHARACTERS

GAVIN   Managing Director of the Chapman and Howard Group, 41

ANDY   Copywriter, 38

BOB   Art Director, 43

PIPPA   Secretary, 19

PATTY   Finance Officer, 44

LEE   Graphic Designer, 22

JO   Accounts Handler, 29

The action of the play takes place in the office of the Chapman and Howard Group, an advertising firm based in Leeds. The time is the present.

ACT ONE

Scene One   Morning, late August.
Scene Two   Night, early September.
Scene Three   Morning, September.
Scene Four   The morning of the party. Early December.
Scene Five   The night of the party.

ACT TWO

Scene One   The night of the party. 11:00 PM.
Scene Two   The morning of the party. 2:00 AM.
Scene Three   The next morning.

ACT ONE

Scene One

The set is a very detailed advertising office. Wharf site. It is early morning. A gantry projects along the upstage area and steps come down left.

PIPPA, *a young woman in her early twenties, is on the phone.*

PIPPA   Good morning, The Chapman and Howard Group. My name is Pippa, how may I help you this morning? I'm sorry, Mr Chapman is busy at the moment. Can I take a message? Ok, thank you.

               (BOB *enters. He is reading a newspaper.*)

BOB   They should bring Boycott back.

               (*Another phone rings.*)

PIPPA   Good morning, The Chapman and Howard Group. My name is Pippa, how may I help you this morning? No, I'm sorry.

BOB   What has happened to cricket in this fuckin' country?

PIPPA   Sure. Can I tell him who called? Yes . . . from? Patterson's. And you are? Right Mr Patterson, thank you for calling, have a nice day.

BOB   We invent the game and then we forget how to play it.

               (PATTY, *a smart woman in her mid-thirties, enters across the upstage area.*)

PATTY   Is he free?

BOB   Here she is.

PATTY   Don't, Bob.

               (*The phone rings.*)

PIPPA	Good morning, The Chapman and Howard Group. My name is Pippa, how may I help you this morning? No, I'm sorry, he doesn't work here any more.
BOB	Was that a call for Maurice?
PIPPA	Yeah.
BOB	That's a bloody miracle. Nobody ever called him when he worked here. Suddenly he leaves and he's Mr Popular.
PATTY	Perhaps you should try that, it might work for you.
BOB	Here she is . . .
PATTY	Is he free? I need to run over these accounts.
PIPPA	He's on his exercise bike. It must have been quite a night, Patty?
PATTY	Not really.
PIPPA	Lucky sod.
PATTY	Spare me.
BOB	I'll go with you next time Pat, you'll be all right with me.
PATTY	Is Andy in?
PIPPA	Late. Again.
BOB	He'll end up in a nut house will that bloke. He takes it all too seriously.
PIPPA	When was the funeral?
PATTY	Three weeks ago.
BOB	The thing is he's too fuckin' strung up, he needs to chill out a bit. I mean she's got him where she wants him. I wouldn't have that.

(ANDY *enters. A man in his late thirties. Attractive but clearly hassled. He looks slightly tired.*)

ANDY   Sorry, shit. Sorry Bob. Sorry. I don't know what's
            happening at the moment. Gooor, honestly. Talk about
            life's rich tapestry. Sorry guys. The alarm didn't go off,
            and then I couldn't find my wallet. Morning everyone
            sorry. My life? Honestly. What is happening? Is he here
            yet?

BOB   Not yet. You need to start taking drugs mate.

ANDY   You reckon?

BOB   It works for Patty.

PIPPA   It's just a sedative isn't it Pat?

BOB   The whole firm's dropping to bits. I'm the only sane one
            here.

            (ANDY *picks up a file from his desk.*)

ANDY   Oh here we go, this is brilliant, this is another line that's
            been doctored. What's he playing at?

            (LEE, *a young and trendy graphic designer, enters.*)

LEE   Coffee?

ANDY   Black. Why do I bother? This is the third copy on the
            trot.

PIPPA   White for me, no sugar.

LEE   Sweet enough, eh?

            (LEE *exits.*)

ANDY   He's power mad.

BOB   I hope I haven't been fuckin' doctored.

PATTY   No, but you ought to be.

ANDY   There speaks a man with five years university research
            behind him.

Bob	Never finished my doctorate . . . couldn't be arsed. Why spend a life studying some boring twat when you can earn more money writing copy.
Andy	Sorry Bob, were you waiting, sorry mate —
Bob	Who picks the English touring squad?
Andy	I can't watch it Bob, it's too exciting.
	(Lee *enters*.)
Pippa	No coffee?
Lee	There's coffee but no cups.
Bob	It's shit coffee anyway.
Lee	I tried to catch some of it in my fingers. I've scalded my hand. Anybody want to suck my fingers? It just kept coming, I didn't know what to do.
Bob	You should have stuck your face under.
Patty	How long have you been here Lee?
Bob	Too long.
Lee	Two weeks.
Bob	Two weeks. That's obscene.
Andy	Two weeks and he's still here.
Lee	I like it.
Bob	How long have you been here?
Pippa	Six months.
Lee	And she still can't make a decent coffee.
Pippa	I can . . .
Bob	I think Gavin puts bromide in the coffee, keeps us on the job.
Patty	Well it doesn't work with you does it?

BOB	It's too early . . .
LEE	He doesn't put bromide in does he?
PIPPA	Come back to Earth, Lee.
ANDY	He might do, I've been feeling distinctly uninterested this last month.
BOB	What does Jenny say to that?
ANDY	Nothing.
BOB	That's dangerous.
ANDY	I know that.
BOB	Losing interest eh?
PATTY	The correct pun would be . . . off the job, Bob.
PIPPA	So where is she?
PATTY	Working out the one-way system?
ANDY	If she is she'll never get here.
PIPPA	Joe Stewart, is he Scottish?
BOB	No, she's lesbian.
ANDY	You reckon?
BOB	Definite, Jo? I mean please, why can't these people have real names?
PATTY	Well she must be good to get Patterson's.
BOB	Did he say how many had applied?
PATTY	Oh come on Bob, I only work here.
LEE	Is Gav married then or what?
PATTY	Was.
PIPPA	Caroline Howard. She ran off with a client.
LEE	Oh right, is that why he mopes about all over the place?

ANDY	Can he say that?
BOB	I think he just did. But as far as we know he's been a good boy ever since, unless Patty knows different?
PATTY	You're very funny Bob, very very funny.
BOB	What have I said now?
PATTY	(*impatient*) Come on Gavin.
LEE	So he's on the lookout then is he?
BOB	Yeh so don't bend over for God's sake.
PATTY	Honestly.
LEE	I bet he's after you Pip?
PIPPA	Chance would be a fine thing . . .
ANDY	Why is it me? Why do I always pull the short straw? I always get landed with some half-baked accounts bozo, who wouldn't know a good copywriter if one stood up and bit them.
BOB	He's a bitter man.
ANDY	I mean I was the one who was landed with Maurice.
PATTY	Lucky you.
ANDY	Bloody Maurice, he never spoke. He nearly bored me to death. And before him there was that fat woman. What a job, eh?
BOB	You worry about it too much, Andy. It's not worth it. It's not a real job anyway.
PATTY	It's not the way you do it.
ANDY	Bloody Maurice, he wore a wig you know? He thought I didn't know. I used to have this sinister desire to knock it off when we were looking at print.
BOB	Well I could've done with that coffee. Didn't they teach you how to get coffee at college?

LEE	I was away that day.
ANDY	Why did he leave?
BOB	Yeh what was wrong with him?
PATTY	What was right with him. He couldn't count for a start.
BOB	Ok, he was a twat but at least he was a quiet twat.
PATTY	Sometimes Bob . . . I think you go a bit too far. There is no need for all that.
BOB	A bit? That's not very mathematical is it?
PATTY	A bit in your case, is a lot . . .
BOB	Come off it Patty. I've heard you in your office effing and blinding into the VDU. Mind you if I had to work out Gavin's expenses I'd swear my fucking head off . . .
PIPPA	You do anyway.
LEE	I read somewhere that someone who swears all the time must have a personality disorder.
ANDY	I think in Bob's case that's true. . .
BOB	Get bollocked.
ANDY	I rest my case your honour . . .
BOB	You ought to be careful with those computers Lee, they're rotting your brain.
LEE	Yeh . . . I'm into virtual reality.
BOB	Your whole life's a virtual reality Lee.
LEE	Eh . . .
BOB	Almost real?
LEE	You should try it Bob, you can have sex and not even get out of the chair.
ANDY	He never does anyway.
BOB	You've been peeping again haven't you?

ANDY	Old habits die hard.
BOB	Right, well I suppose I'd better go and find a tea bag to suck on.

(BOB *exits. As he does,* GAVIN *enters. A striking man in his late thirties. The laughter is slightly cut by* GAVIN'S *entrance.*)

GAVIN	Morning all . . .
ALL	Morning.
GAVIN	(*loaded*) Sorry Pat, have you been waiting?
PATTY	No, no not really.
GAVIN	Jo's not here then?
LEE	Might have got lost.
GAVIN	Lee I don't care what you do sunshine, but look like you're doing something, all right?
LEE	Right, yeh right.
GAVIN	What can you tell me?
LEE	Graphics are done, and the coffee machines knackered?
GAVIN	Well fix it.
LEE	Oh right.
GAVIN	Any messages?
PIPPA	Patterson's. Mr P himself. He'll call back.
GAVIN	Oh Pippa, do me a favour don't dress like that — no one'll want to marry you, will they Lee?
LEE	Oh I dunno . . .
ANDY	Any chance of discussing this, Gav?

(ANDY *refers to his doctored document.*)

GAVIN	Yeh, I liked it but it's too busy.

ANDY	Well we could . . .
GAVIN	It's good stuff . . .
ANDY	Yeh but . . .
GAVIN	It's great. I love it.
ANDY	I just erm . . . if we could.
GAVIN	Not right now.
ANDY	Ok, yeh great.
GAVIN	But we need the Patterson thing.
ANDY	Yeh yeh . . .
GAVIN	Right ready?
PATTY	Yeh, yeh. Always ready.
GAVIN	Right, let's see what the VAT man's after . . .
PATTY	It's not good.
GAVIN	Is it ever?

(GAVIN *and* PATTY *enter* GAVIN'S *office.* LEE *still lingers.* ANDY *goes to his desk.*)

PIPPA	Oooh, icy.
LEE	Am I missing something here?
PIPPA	Hey you!
LEE	What?
PIPPA	Coffee machine. Fix it.

(ANDY, *dejected, sits at his desk. Looks at a newspaper.*)

ANDY	Oh this bloody job.
PIPPA	Are you ok?
ANDY	Me? Oh, I'm fine. Fine. Never been better.

(BOB *enters*.)

BOB   The milk's off.

PIPPA   There's some more in the fridge.

BOB   Good thinking.

               (ANDY *is transfixed by an article in the paper*.)

ANDY   Oh have you seen this?

BOB   You shouldn't be reading that, you're not ready for it.

ANDY   Two kids of eleven have raped a ten year old.

BOB   I saw that.

ANDY   What the fu . . . Eh? I didn't know what sex was when I was eleven. I was worrying about my eleven plus.

BOB   What happened in Brum then?

ANDY   Jeeesuuu.

PIPPA   She hasn't said anything.

BOB   Oh yeh. Ken West reckoned they were very cosy, he saw them in the Hyatt.

ANDY   I thought Patty was on your list Bob.

BOB   I'm working my way through the secretaries first.

PIPPA   You're what?

BOB   You know who we're bidding against, don't you?

ANDY   Not Caroline?

BOB   She set up on her own.

ANDY   Since when?

BOB   It's a good set up apparently. I've thought about going over . . .

               (LEE *enters*.)

LEE	No good, it's completely knackered. We'll have to get someone in. I haven't got a clue.
PIPPA	You're right here.
LEE	I've got to get on with the Aqua Vac. Is that yours?
ANDY	No that's one of Mr Marsden's.
BOB	Another work of genius. This time it's vacuum cleaners. Is there no end to this man's talents?

(LEE *is about to depart when* JO, *a striking woman in her late twenties, extremely confident, sexy and pugnacious, enters.*)

JO	Hiya, sorry.
BOB	Why, what have you done?
JO	It's a nightmare getting through town.
BOB	It's a nightmare getting anywhere around here. I think they're digging the city up.
ANDY	Yeh, it's the council, they're trying to escape. They've spent the money, now they're running.
PIPPA	Can I help you?
JO	I hope so. I'm Jo.

(*Silence.*)

BOB	Eh?
JO	Jo Stewart.
BOB	Oh fuck me.
JO	No thanks.
ANDY	Bob for God's sake.
BOB	You're not Scottish then?
JO	Sorry?
BOB	I'm Bob. This is Andy.

Jo	Yeh, Gavin said . . .
Bob	Oh been talking about us, has he?
Jo	Just the descriptions.
Bob	And was he close?
Jo	I think he . . .
Bob	When he described me, did he use the phrase, Sex God at all?
Jo	No I don't think he did actually.
Bob	Joke, Jo, joke . . . that's all.

(Bob *stands to shake* Jo's *hand*.)

Bob	Are you all right for a coffee, Jo?
Jo	Great.
Lee	There is none.
Jo	Well it's the thought that counts.
Bob	Tea?
Jo	Tea would be nice.
Bob	Tea would be nice wouldn't it?
Lee	I'll get it Bob, you stay in your chair.
Bob	It's no trouble. I'll just whip up a quick cuppa. You'd better get cracking on the Aqua Vac. They're going to need that for Friday's meeting. Chop chop young man, let's see some action.

(Lee *is about to exit.*)

Lee	I'm Lee. Graphics.

(*He exits.*)

Bob	Tea darling?
Andy	Two sugars.

BOB	Nice and sweet, just how I like it.
	(BOB *exits. An awkward moment.* PIPPA *stands and collects some papers.*)
PIPPA	I'd better pop these down to production before they lynch me.
JO	You do that.
PIPPA	Welcome to the madhouse.
	(PIPPA *exits. Silence.*)
JO	So, right.
ANDY	Right, do you want to . . . ?
JO	Where am I?
ANDY	Corridor, second right.
JO	Right well . . .
ANDY	I suppose Gavin'll do the big intro . . . er . . . well . . .
JO	I suppose.
ANDY	. . . introduce everyone.
JO	Yeh.
ANDY	Well . . . welcome, welcome.
JO	Thank you.
ANDY	Up from the Smoke, eh?
JO	That's right.
ANDY	Well we won't bite. Contrary to popular myth.
JO	I'm sure you won't.
ANDY	Up from the Smoke.
JO	Is there a problem?

ANDY	No, no . . . we were guessing what you'd be like, and nobody really got it right. Erm, you're bit different to Maurice.
JO	Maurice?
ANDY	Bald bloke, wore a wig, we did great things with patio doors. Boring really, Jo. No matter. So well, running shoes?
JO	Supposed to be the best.
ANDY	I wouldn't know Jo, I just try to sell the bloody things.
JO	I'm looking forward to it.
ANDY	It'll be rivetting I'm sure.
JO	He told me you'd been here a long time.
ANDY	I'm past my best though.
JO	That's not what I hear.
ANDY	Every line I write Gavin alters.
JO	Shame.
ANDY	He says if I want to write sentences I should write a novel.
JO	That's good.
ANDY	Oh yeh, I'm a natural, they drop out of me.
JO	Well I'm looking forward to working with you.
	(BOB *enters with tea for himself and* JO.)
BOB	Tea.
JO	Lovely.
ANDY	Where's mine?
BOB	In the kitchen.
ANDY	Cheers. Yeh we're a great team Jo, as you can see.

(ANDY *exits towards the kitchen.*)

BOB   Well best of health, Jo. Pity it's not stronger, eh?

JO   That's right.

BOB   That's right. Absolutely.

JO   (*sipping her tea*) Mmmm, lovely.

BOB   Well cheers. All the best.

JO   Yeh.

BOB   (*sipping tea, loaded*) Mmm, lovely.

JO   Mmmm.

BOB   Yeh.

JO   Just what I needed.

BOB   And me.

JO   There's nothing quite like it.

BOB   Absolutely . . .

(BOB *laughs.* JO *nods nervously. Both laugh. Music.*)

Scene Two

One month later. Night. The office is dim, with strong shadows and glowing lights from outside. LEE *enters the main office. He puts on his coat.*

LEE   Oh man, Bob is crazy.

ANDY   Why, what's he done now?

LEE   I think he must be addicted to photocopier fluid? He's always in there.

ANDY   Have you finished the Vita Pet image?

LEE   Yeh, it's good and all.

ANDY   What is it?

LEE	I've got this dog, right, cartoon, with a big shiny nose looking towards you, looking really healthy, and smiling. It's got it's head just to one side. Ears all floppy. It's brilliant.
ANDY	This isn't a job for a grown man is it?
LEE	Well it makes me laugh.

(BOB *enters, ready for home.*)

BOB	Right that's another one down the pan, fancy a pint?
ANDY	No . . . I'm —
BOB	You staying late again? What's got into you, you're usually the first one away?
ANDY	Got to finish this . . .
LEE	Oh yeh?
ANDY	For God's sake.
LEE	She doesn't even talk to me. I'm not important enough.
BOB	Lucky sod.
ANDY	Eh?
BOB	And I thought it was me she was after.
ANDY	What's up, are you jealous?
BOB	Be careful.
ANDY	Dear me . . .
BOB	I tell you this — she's a bit of all right.
ANDY	Well thank you Desmond Morris.
BOB	No, I'm serious. I'm pleased it's you she's working with, I couldn't stand the stress. I'd get ideas. She'd only have to smile at me and I'd be getting my kit off.
LEE	Nice one.
BOB	You'll be on the filing cabinet in no time.

ANDY   I don't think so.

BOB   You know why he wanted her?

ANDY   Because she's good.

BOB   Yeh. But who does she remind you of?

ANDY   I dunno.

BOB   Caroline.

ANDY   Does she hell . . .

BOB   She does, she looks like Caroline Howard.

ANDY   Bob, I think you're falling for her.

BOB   She's the spitting image.

ANDY   She's just a woman, let her get on with it.

BOB   (*mock*) And you're a man, she looked into his deep blue eyes and knew there's was a passion bursting to express itself.

ANDY   You're in the wrong job.

BOB   No, I've just discovered I'm in the right fucking job.

ANDY   So we've got a suit and she's a woman. It's the 1920's.

BOB   Don't tell me you haven't fantasised about her already because I don't believe you.

LEE   Bob you should write novels. You're wasted here.

BOB   It's only natural, what're you worried about?

ANDY   You reading the wrong books.

BOB   I don't think so.

ANDY   Go and have a beer Bob, cool off a bit. And put some of it down your pants.

BOB   Is she married then or what?

LEE	He's probably one of the Gladiators.
BOB	Just my fucking luck.
ANDY	The poor woman has only been here two weeks and you and Gavin are ogling her all the time. No wonder she's tetchy. Just back off and give her some space.
BOB	That's a bad sign Andy, over-protective workmate.
ANDY	Honestly? Are things with you and Cath so bad? I mean come on?
BOB	And you've got the best marriage in the world have you?
ANDY	Just forget it shall we?
BOB	No, go on what were you going to say?
ANDY	Nothing. I don't want to get into an argument.
BOB	An argument about what?
	(JO *enters lightly.*)
JO	I was down there waiting . . .
ANDY	Oh right.
JO	Hi.
BOB	Hiya.
JO	Working late aren't you?
BOB	Just finishing off a few things. I was just saying to Andy it's a shame you've both got to work late. We could have a beer. Anyway, we'd better get off, Lee.
LEE	That's right.
BOB	See you tomorrow.
LEE	Yeh, sleep tight.
BOB	They're not going to work that late are you?
JO	I shouldn't think so.

LEE	Night-night.
	(BOB *and* LEE *exit*.)
JO	What was all that about?
ANDY	It's just Bob. He's got a funny sense of humour.
JO	What, like he hasn't got one?
ANDY	He's got one but it's vicious.
JO	You should see mine.
ANDY	I'd rather not. I'm more interested in the quiet life these days.
JO	You're talking like an old man.
ANDY	I can see forty looming large.
JO	I thought life began at forty?
ANDY	So they say. I think I've just mellowed. In fact if I get any more mellow, I'll be rotten.
JO	That's quite good.
ANDY	It's a disease Jo. I speak to my kids in ad lines.
JO	We should be through this by ten.
ANDY	Ten? I was banking on half eight.
JO	Well you go, but I'll . . .
ANDY	If it's ten it's ten.
JO	If it's a problem?
ANDY	No. I get a bit of needle every now and again. Jenny reckons I'm married to Chapman and Howard.
JO	I know the feeling.
ANDY	It doesn't really matter what time I get back, dinner's in the fridge anyway.
JO	A boil-in-the-bag man are you?

ANDY   It's Healthy Options actually. Jenny thinks I need to lose
          a stone.

JO   Oh.

ANDY   Story of my life. I've always got to lose something.

JO   You look all right . . .

ANDY   That's what I think. But she's right. It's got to come off.

JO   Join a gym, that's what I did. I only use the sauna
          though, all that stuff's to energetic for me.

ANDY   I did do. Joining it was the easy bit. It's the mindless
          jogging that gets me.

JO   I just sit and sweat it out.

ANDY   Yeh but Jo, I'd be in there for days. Look at you, I've
          seen more fat on a chip.

JO   Is that a compliment or what?

ANDY   Actually I should lose a stone, but you know what it's
          like. I had a stress test last year. I didn't even get on the
          fitness graph. My blood pressure's ok, my heart beats,
          but in terms of fitness I don't exist.

JO   Don't die on me.

ANDY   I'll do my best.

JO   You know Gavin thinks very highly of you?

ANDY   Get off.

JO   So he says.

ANDY   Oh well.

JO   So there you go.

ANDY   I'm thinking of having a change to be honest.

JO   Why?

ANDY   Ten years in the same place and you start to feel like it's time to move on.

JO   Ten years? That's a long time.

ANDY   Tell me about it. Two years ago we moved into a bigger house. Jenny wanted a study. I should have an arrangement with the Abbey National, so that everything I earn goes to them. Have you seen my car? Gooor. I'm trapped Jo, trapped. I've even thought about selling the kids.

JO   How many?

ANDY   How many or how much?

JO   You don't stop do you?

ANDY   I thought you were making me an offer.

JO   Oh no.

ANDY   Two. One of each. Do you have any?

JO   No.

ANDY   You wait . . .

JO   That's right . . .

ANDY   Your career goes right out of the window.

JO   I'll have to wait and see.

ANDY   Mind you, you'll probably cope. You're one of those who's good at everything aren't you? Go on admit it.

JO   Not everything.

ANDY   Well enjoy it while you can, because the older you get the more it all falls to bits.

JO   It's not that different being thirty-eight is it? I mean I'm not a kid. Let's be honest.

ANDY   Do you still have your parents?

JO   Yes. I don't see them much but . . .

ANDY	That's the difference.
Jo	Well yeh.
ANDY	My mother died a month ago. It's a weird one. My dad is an absolute wreck. Whooophh. Since then I've been all over the place with my nerves. Panic attacks. Have you had them?
Jo	I don't think so.
ANDY	You'd know. It's like dying only worse.
Jo	How come?
ANDY	You only die once. I have these every week. Anyway. So I've started taking homeopathic pills but I panic because I think they're addictive. Rescue Remedy, Kalms, you name it. Jenny thinks I'm having a breakdown. I think she might be right.
Jo	Well you're making me feel ill.
ANDY	I've got this thing about my heart now. I think I'm going to have a heart attack. I get these pains across my chest. Tingling down my arms. It's probably indigestion, but you never know. I've seen a consultant, he reckons it's stress. It cost me a hundred and sixty quid for him to tell me I'm stressed. I could've told him that myself. That's why I joined the gym. Now I think I'm going to have a stroke on the treadmill.
Jo	How long have you been married?
ANDY	Thirteen years. What about you?
Jo	Two.
ANDY	Two? You're still on honeymoon.
Jo	I don't think so.
ANDY	What does he do?
Jo	He works in the City. It's not a fancy job. But . . .
ANDY	So he hasn't moved up?

Jo	He can't, I'm only renting anyway. So weekends, you know? Back down.
Andy	You're not going to be here long are you?
Jo	Oh, you're trying to get rid of me already.
Andy	No I'm not. I wouldn't dream of it. But you up here and him . . . I mean, you know? You might end up having panic attacks.
Jo	Well we could both turn to drink.
Andy	No I've tried that, it doesn't work. I worry too much about my bloody blood pressure.
Jo	Well I think we'd better get at it.
Andy	Yeh, before I completely fall to bits.
Jo	Right.
Andy	I'll just give Jenny a quick er . . .
Jo	Priorities.
Andy	Absolutely.

(Jo *exits.* Andy *phones.*)

Andy   Hi Jess, it's Daddy. Is Mummy there? Is she? Can she come to the phone? Have you? That's good. And has Grandad been doing it as well? Good. No Grandma won't. No. Is Mummy coming? Is she? Well let me speak to her then darling? Yeh soon. No you'll be in bed. Ok? And I love you too. (Jenny *is on the line.*) Hi it's me. Everything all right? Yeh. Yeh. Look, it's going to be another late one. Yeh, yeh, yeh I know that, but what can I do? I'll pack it in then shall I? I'm not being stupid. Oh look, I didn't ring up for an argument. Sorry, yeh. About eleven, could be before. Bob's gone, you know Bob? Jo Stewart. That's right. Jenny? I don't know what Bob does, nobody knows what Bob does, what does it matter I'm here, Jenny, Jen?

(Jenny *has hung up.* Andy *replaces the receiver. He is heavy with guilt.* Jo *enters with a chilled beer.*)

Jo	Everything ok?
ANDY	Yeh fine. No problem.
Jo	Great.
ANDY	Yeh, home sweet home.
Jo	Would you panic if I gave you one of these?

(Jo *shows* ANDY *a can of Budweiser.*)

ANDY	Just what the doctor ordered.

(Jo *throws the can to* ANDY.)

Jo	Right then, let's get at it. All the visuals are up here.

(Jo *climbs the stairs towards the graphics office.* ANDY
*cannot help but watch her as she mounts the steps. She
is sexy without knowing it.* ANDY *stands and watches her
go. He looks at the can of beer, opens it and it sprays all
over him.*)

ANDY	Oh shit.

(*Music. Blackout.*)

Scene Three

A few days later, morning. GAVIN *is prowling around the office. He is
slightly anxious. He looks at the odd desk.* PIPPA *enters, she is wearing
a very short skirt. She hands* GAVIN *a cup of coffee.*

GAVIN	Ahh . . . thank you.
PIPPA	A life saver, aren't I?
GAVIN	Absolutely.
PIPPA	Yeh I feel a bit rough myself.
GAVIN	Late night?
PIPPA	I had a party. Been trying to arrange it for the last three weeks. My Mother's in Spain. Thank God.

GAVIN   Good was it?

PIPPA   No not really. Everybody thought it was going to be
             wild but we just sat about and talked 'till four. I don't
             think any of us had the guts to make the first move.
             Boring really.

GAVIN   Oh right, and I'd got you down as a raver.

PIPPA   Me, I am, but there was nobody to rave with.

GAVIN   Can we get somebody to come and clear up the foyer?
             It's like a bloody tip down there. Looks like some
             dosser's been using it to sleep in.

PIPPA   Smells awful doesn't it?

GAVIN   Tell the cleaners to come and get it sorted or we'll find a
             new contractor.

PIPPA   They're sleeping all over the place along the bank, you
             can see 'em in the mornings. Shall I phone the police?

             (LEE *enters from the interior office. He has a coffee.*)

LEE   It works then?

PIPPA   Ninety quid to fix it.

LEE   Do I need a pen for this meeting, or will I be able to
             remember it?

GAVIN   Be on the safe side Lee, get a pen.

LEE   A pen, right.

GAVIN   Have you got a place of your own yet?

LEE   Not yet.

GAVIN   Still looking?

LEE   Yeh.

GAVIN   So the parties have started early this year?

PIPPA   Christmas gets earlier every year.

(LEE *scrounges around, but can only come up with a pencil.*)

LEE   Will a pencil do?

               (PATTY *enters.*)

PATTY   What's happening?

GAVIN   Good question.

PATTY   Are we meeting in here or shall I get them all in the boardroom?

GAVIN   In here.

PATTY   Right. Oh Rothwell's been on.

GAVIN   Don't tell me.

PATTY   Overdraft facility. He's going to blow a gasket.

GAVIN   Lee's still looking for a place, Pat.

PATTY   Sorry?

GAVIN   I think he wants to create a love nest.

LEE   Chance would be a fine thing.

PATTY   No. Jo?

GAVIN   Or Andy.

PATTY   Arrr . . .

GAVIN   What?

PATTY   They must've been here till late?

GAVIN   Well I hope it's worth it.

LEE   There's something going on there.

GAVIN   No . . .

LEE   Maybe it's me. I've got a ridiculous imagination.

GAVIN   What do you think Pat?

PATTY   Not Andy . . .

(BOB *enters with a cup of tea. His cup is filthy.*)

BOB	What's happening to the cleaners?
GAVIN	We're onto it.
BOB	This is dangerous.
PIPPA	You should've got a clean one.
BOB	This is a clean one. The others have got fuckin' aliens growing from them.
GAVIN	Bob, can I say, Aqua Vac.
BOB	Yes you can.
GAVIN	And Regatta.
BOB	Nearly done.
GAVIN	It's just that I want to submit it this year.
BOB	Oh, this year.
GAVIN	Can I say, soon Bob.
BOB	I hear you.
GAVIN	Soon Bob. That means like, very very soon.

(*A very annoyed* JO *and a very hassled* ANDY *arrive.*)

JO	Sorry.
BOB	Here they are . . .
JO	Sorry everyone. Gav, sorry.
GAVIN	Arrr.
JO	I hate being late.
PATTY	We were beginning to wonder.
BOB	Why don't you two just sleep here, I think it'll save all this hassle?
ANDY	Sorry everyone.

GAVIN	Well I hope this is going to be worth it?
JO	So do we. Patterson's changed his mind fifty times.
ANDY	It was my fault. I said that I'd give Jo a lift, and the bloody car conked out. I tried to push the damn thing and it set off a panic do. Jeesuu. Sorry.
PATTY	Oh Andy . . .
JO	I'm sat there, didn't know what . . .
ANDY	Sorry.
JO	I thought he'd had it. I was looking around for him, but I couldn't . . .
ANDY	I was just sat in the road . . .
GAVIN	Anyway . . .
ANDY	Sorry. I feel bloody pathetic . . . ugh.
BOB	I told you not to read the papers didn't I?
ANDY	Why me though? I was as fit as a butcher's dog once.
LEE	It must be your age?
ANDY	I get flushed then my heart races. I tell you this, you feel as if you're going to die . . .
BOB	Well I always live every day as my last, because I know that one of these days I'm going to be right.
ANDY	Thanks Bob, very reassuring.
JO	I was just sat hugging him, in the middle of the road.
ANDY	She was great but . . .
GAVIN	Right, well. At least you're all in one piece.
BOB	Just.

(*Silence.*)

GAVIN	Look I don't want to sound like a misery. And I'm saying this to every department. So don't think it's just you.
BOB	You mean we're not special?

(*Laughter.*)

GAVIN	Well?
PIPPA	Oh, I thought we were . . .
GAVIN	You know I've got a soft spot, but I'm being serious now.
BOB	Shame.
GAVIN	Serious. I know that you look at all this and you think we are coining it in. Am I right?
BOB	Would we ever think anything like that?
JO	Probably.

(*Laughter.*)

GAVIN	And everyone thinks Gavin must be loaded.
LEE	Lend a quid . . .
GAVIN	Very good, Nero.
BOB	Actually how many million are you worth Gav?
GAVIN	I wish I was.

(*A big groan.*)

GAVIN	Seriously. We read in the papers about those little green shoots, and we think we are in clover. Well we're not folks. The water is rising, and we're struggling to keep our necks above the water line. And I read about us all coming out of recession but it's going to be a long slow haul. And you know I'll do what I can to fight redundancies but we've all got to pull the same way, and we're cut to the bone as it is. And everybody knows that we like a laugh in this office. I mean, come on, it's like a bloody riot in here half the time. Isn't it Bob?

BOB   Discrimination.

GAVIN   And everybody knows I like to keep things nice and
           friendly, but enough ladies and gents is frankly enough.
           It's not easy to say this. Some of you have been here
           right from the start. And I know it sounds petty, and
           I've been as guilty as some of you in the past. But can
           we seriously stop wasting paper? Last quarter's bill was
           just ludicrous, and I'm not big on the tree thing, and I
           haven't suddenly gone green.

JO   Which is a pity.

GAVIN   Fair point. But it's getting beyond a joke. There's
           memo's plastered all over downstairs. Some of them
           are just insane. Memo's like, and I quote, "Fat Busters
           every Thursday — see Patty".

PATTY   Sorry.

GAVIN   "Stop press, it's official, Lee is an alien".

PIPPA   It's the truth . . .

           (*Laughter.*)

GAVIN   And somebody has done a broadsheet on A5 paper
           which is just ridiculous.

BOB   Lee.

GAVIN   It complains of someone leaving an enormous turd in
           the side of the pan in one of the gent's bogs.

BOB   That is Lee.

GAVIN   Well whoever it was, somebody thought it was amusing
           because there've been several replies to it. One of them
           said it was cruel to draw attention to this as it might be
           a person who's arsehole isn't in the usual cleft between
           the buttock but on the buttock itself. Oh yes I've read
           them all. Another one suggested that all the afflicted
           person had to do was move slightly off the seat so that
           the offending buttock was right across the water.

LEE   Who did that one . . .

GAVIN   Yeah, it's very funny.

(All the office find this amusing. BOB *has produced this and everyone knows it.* ANDY *is still gently recovering.)*

Laugh, yeh. Two hundred and thirty pounds worth of photocopying materials isn't that right Pat?

PATTY   Yes.

GAVIN   Not to mention, electricity, man hours. That's your wage Lee.

LEE   Just about.

GAVIN   We can't afford it. It's funny, it's creative but nobody'll buy it. And can I remind the person who has been phoning the '0898' chatline that all our telephone calls are metered and traced. So pack it in Bob.

BOB   It's not me honest. I've tried 'em they don't do a thing for me. It's Patty.

GAVIN   Yeh well. Thanks for your time folks. Oh and by the way, because of the recession the party will be limited to one bottle of red and fifty straws.

(Everyone boos. GAVIN *disappears towards his office.* JO *exits.* PATTY *follows* GAVIN.)

PATTY   Gavin, don't forget Mr Rothwell . . .

GAVIN   I won't.

*(*PIPPA *returns to her post.* LEE *is about to depart.)*

BOB   Put the kettle on, sunbeam.

LEE   Can we afford it?

*(*LEE *exits.)*

ANDY   There was no need for all that was there?

BOB   That's because you were late.

ANDY   Why, is he jealous?

BOB   He might not be.

ANDY	Oh give up man.
BOB	Hugging you in the street, eh?
ANDY	She didn't know what to do did she?
BOB	I think I might start having panic attacks. It's a good angle.
ANDY	Hey listen Bob . . .
BOB	Very useful . . .
ANDY	Listen, honestly I don't want to fall out with you, but pack it in, ok?
BOB	What?
ANDY	Oh come on.
BOB	Don't get heavy.
ANDY	I'm not.
BOB	Oooh eh . . .
ANDY	No Bob, please . . .
BOB	What's up?
ANDY	I don't want it at the moment.
BOB	Oh come on it's only . . . /
ANDY	. . . / I just don't want it ok?
BOB	What's wrong with you?
ANDY	Nothing.
BOB	Nobody can talk to you without you giving a fit.
ANDY	All I'm saying is give it a rest, because people start to get the wrong idea.
BOB	Like who?
ANDY	Well.
BOB	Who?

ANDY	Anybody.
BOB	Nobody's interested.
ANDY	People gossip.
BOB	I'm only giving a laugh Andy.
ANDY	I know but?
BOB	I'm only having a laugh.
ANDY	Yeh well it's not funny.

(BOB *walks away from* ANDY, *getting on with his work.*)

BOB	It is to me mate. It fucking is to me.

(ANDY *reluctantly sets to work. Music plays, lights fade.*)

Scene Four

The office. Winter. The morning of the party. It is a crisp, cold day outside. JO *is in the office,* ANDY *is clutching onto a plastic coffee. It is burning his fingers. He demonstrates this to* JO. *The office is distinctly quiet.*

JO	Is it hot?
ANDY	No it's heavy. Mind you I'm a quick learner, I only get burnt the once.
JO	Are you sure?

(ANDY *gives* JO *a coffee. It burns her.*)

JO	Arrggh, you're right.
ANDY	Told you.
JO	Well at least they like the campaign. Thank God.
ANDY	I should hope so.
JO	We should start running it in February.
ANDY	I still think we should have gone with "the ultimate".

Jo	No way.
ANDY	I mean, how wimpy, "put a spring in your step". Come on!
Jo	They're paying for it.
ANDY	I could just picture it. Posters all over the country. Fifty foot high, with one pair of Patterson's pumps and nothing else, and then, across the bottom, bold black on white. Simply "the ultimate . . ." Nothing else. There is no other shoe even worth thinking about.
Jo	No way, it's too butch.
ANDY	Listen I'd buy something called the ultimate, I'm that gullible.
Jo	You said it.
ANDY	I am. I buy Mars bars because you can work, rest and play. Doesn't say anything about getting as fat as a bastard.
Jo	Not just a pretty face are you?
ANDY	Not even.
Jo	Oh I don't know. I think you've got a nice face.
ANDY	Get away.
Jo	You won't let anybody flatter you.
ANDY	I will, I'm just not used to it.
Jo	Give over, I bet Jenny's at it all the time.

(*A moment's repose.*)

ANDY	So tonight's the night.
Jo	Not for me. It's a bottle of wine and a video I'm afraid.
ANDY	If you don't go Gavin takes it personal.
Jo	Tough. Is Jenny going?

ANDY   Not after last year.

JO   Can't she take the pace?

ANDY   It's very much a spectator sport. I'm taking my
            Wellingtons.

JO   It get's kinky does it?

ANDY   Ooooh . . .

JO   What is it, a bring-a-shovel party?

ANDY   We could've done with one last year, the shit was up
            here. (*Gestures*.) Gav and Caroline decided it was time
            to open a vein. They took bits off each other. Patty
            wanted to call the police. Jenny left, Cathy left, half of
            marketing legged it. I only stayed because it was my
            turn to give Bob a lift, he was loving it. That's when
            they decided to call it a day. So this year there's no
            wives or girlfriends or anything complicated.

JO   Neil couldn't come anyway. It's their party tonight.

ANDY   You should go there.

JO   I hate parties. If I don't go to his I can't really come
            here.

ANDY   It's just Vivaldi and a sausage on a stick.

JO   Oh, I thought there was a disco?

ANDY   There is, worse luck. The DJ's the kid with one eye
            from the Star.

JO   Oh God, it sounds awful.

ANDY   It will be if I start dancing. I'm likely to poke
            somebody's eye out. That's why I don't dance. I'm
            dangerous. I'm banned from every disco in Leeds.

JO   Disco king, eh?

ANDY   No that's Bob. Two years ago we had an oriental theme.
            He came as a Sumo wrestler. He was naked on the
            tables at eleven o'clock.

Jo	I think I can live without seeing that.
ANDY	Right, I'd better see how far Lee's got.

(ANDY *exits as* PIPPA *enters from the stairs.*)

PIPPA	Oh he's in a mood today. And he's usually nice, don't you think?
Jo	(*with humour*) No.
PIPPA	Don't you think?
Jo	Not my type.
PIPPA	Don't you think he's just a bit dishy?
Jo	Too smooth for me.
PIPPA	Let's be honest, there's not a lot of choice here is there? I mean, I don't hold much hope out for tonight. I mean look at dirty Bob, who's going to get landed with him?
Jo	It might be your lucky night.
PIPPA	I'm going stay with the production lot, there's more life.
Jo	Now they are sad.

(PATTY *has entered, with a large file.*)

PATTY	Who's sad?
PIPPA	Bob the blob.
PATTY	Oh sad or bad? Or both.
Jo	Is he married?
PATTY	Four kids.
Jo	Bob the blob is a dark horse then?
PATTY	Two of each. Nice kids actually. Andy's got two. I've got two, Ted Payne's got five . . . So there you go, better get cracking.
Jo	Not for me.

PATTY	That's what they all say.
JO	No I mean it.
PATTY	They're the best thing to happen to you. Believe me, it's the only thing to have faith in.
JO	Yeh I know that but . . . it's just one of those things.
PATTY	Oh sorry. I never . . .
JO	You can't have everything.
PATTY	I just assumed.
JO	Yeh well . . .
PATTY	Ooooh . . .
JO	It's ok Patty, I feel ok about it, I mean it's not a disease or anything. Could be worse.
PATTY	Oh I feel awful.
JO	It just means I don't go in Mothercare a lot. Well I do go in actually. I buy my sister's kids everything there is. We spoil them rotten. It's a good job we don't have any. We wouldn't have any cash.
PATTY	I'm sorry, you know?
PIPPA	I wonder how she sleeps with him?
PATTY	Who?
PIPPA	I'm still on Bob's wife.
PATTY	I don't think she does.
JO	Probably thought better of it.
PATTY	Well he's been seeing a woman in town for as long as I've been here.
JO	You're joking?
PATTY	Whenever he says he's popping out for a sandwich, he means he's going for a bit of whatever. He came

back once with his track suit bottoms on inside-out.
You should've seen him trying to explain that one. Gav
followed him one day, said she's quite nice apparently,
works in Binns.

JO   There's no wonder he can't stand still.

PATTY   The thing is, she's called Cathy, so whenever Cathy
            rings up, Bob starts sweating.

JO   I bet he does.

PATTY   You should see him at the party — he's like an octopus.

PIPPA   What's it like?

            (ANDY *enters from the interior office*.)

PATTY   What's the party like Andy?

ANDY   I was telling Jo, bedlam. A tonic water and I'm off.

PATTY   Shall I tell 'em about the cup?

ANDY   (*looking for a file*) I can't stand it.

PIPPA   What is it?

ANDY   (*finds the file*) Ah, I'd forget my head if it was loose.

PATTY   Well after last year's party somebody found a cup in the
            board room.

ANDY   Don't, I can't stand it.

PATTY   And it was full of, you know?

PIPPA   What?

PATTY   We think it was Ingrid and Ken West. She chooses
            somebody at the beginning of the night and woof —
            goes for it.

ANDY   Ugh no. I can't stand it, civilization is crumbling. Come
            back Christmas, all is forgiven.

            (ANDY *exits with the file*.)

PATTY	They just left it on the table.
PIPPA	Who's cup was it?
JO	Probably Bob's?

(GAVIN *enters, rather touchy.*)

GAVIN	Am I going insane or did those figures get to Patterson's?
JO	Yes.
GAVIN	Oh.
JO	Is there a problem? Did they receive them?
PIPPA	Yeh, I checked.
GAVIN	I said you'd take them around that's all.
JO	There was no point, was there?
GAVIN	Yes there was.
PIPPA	They have got them.
GAVIN	It's just that I said that you would take them.
JO	I didn't see the point.
GAVIN	The point is, I said that you would take them around personally. I gave my word that you would deliver them. I've just had Patterson on telling me that we might not be able to do business.
JO	Well I'm sorry, I didn't think . . .
GAVIN	You didn't think?
JO	Of course I thought —
GAVIN	And what if we lose the account?
JO	Because I didn't take them?
GAVIN	Well this is what he's saying to me.
JO	Well if you must know the man is a right little shit.

GAVIN	Is he?
PATTY	I'll be in finance if anybody . . . erm.

(PATTY *exits*.)

JO	I'm sorry, but yes he is.
GAVIN	Not as sorry as I'll be.
JO	I thought it would ok.
GAVIN	Well it's not.
JO	I can see that.
GAVIN	Right.
JO	Right.
GAVIN	So maybe next time you'll do exactly as I say?
JO	Obviously.
GAVIN	Good.
JO	There was a reason you know.
GAVIN	Oh well that's good. I'm pleased there was a reason. I suppose you'd better enlighten us.
JO	Second thoughts, I don't think I will . . . not here.
GAVIN	I think you should.
JO	Do you think we could talk about this privately?

(*A phone rings.* PIPPA *answers it*.)

PIPPA	The Chapman and Howard Group.
GAVIN	I've got workmen in my office, the bank having a fit. Now all I want to know is why have I got this man shouting down the phone at me when all I asked you to do was humour him a bit?
JO	Humour him?
GAVIN	Oh, come on.

Jo	He loves himself.
GAVIN	He ought to do, for God's sake he's worth a fortune.
PIPPA	Gavin, it's Mr Rothwell from the bank.
GAVIN	I'm not in. I'll call him back.
PIPPA	Hello Mr Rothwell, Mr Chapman's not available at the moment. Can I get him to call you back?
GAVIN	Pippa, make a couple of coffees will you?
	(PIPPA *exits unwillingly*.)
	Thanks. Ok?
Jo	Every meeting I've had with Patterson he's come on a bit strong.
GAVIN	He's like that.
Jo	The man is right out of order.
GAVIN	I thought you could deal with anybody?
Jo	Oh you're really good . . .
GAVIN	He's a bit touchy, I know.
Jo	Oh, come on?
GAVIN	Play the game . . .
Jo	What?
GAVIN	You know what . . .
Jo	Oh, very good.
GAVIN	Are you saying he made a pass?
Jo	A pass? A pass I can deal with, the man's a sodding head case.
GAVIN	So what, so what are you saying?
Jo	I'm saying that he was trying to get into my pants that's what I'm saying. And then he asked me if I wanted to fuck him!

GAVIN	And what did you say?
Jo	What could I?
GAVIN	So you didn't say no?
Jo	No.
GAVIN	Oh.
Jo	Not in so many words.
GAVIN	Oh right.
Jo	Well, I mean . . .
GAVIN	So presumably he thought . . .
Jo	I don't know what he thought.
GAVIN	Oh, come on.
Jo	You come on.
GAVIN	You should've told him to stuff it.
Jo	Yeh.
GAVIN	And is that it?
Jo	No.
GAVIN	So.
Jo	He sends for a car, we get in. And I think ok fine, he's got the message, great. One to him. I'll put it down to experience. But then he gets his thing out. I couldn't believe it. He's just sat there grinning. I look out of the window, anywhere, but not at him. And then he says, "There's no chance of a little suck is there? Come on, put your mouth on it. Come on, if you won't fuck me suck me."
GAVIN	Right . . .
Jo	And while he's offering me this little taster his hands are all over me.

GAVIN   Right, I think I've got it . . .

JO   No you haven't got it, you haven't got the half of it. So
             I ask the driver to stop and I walked all the way back up
             here. Now I haven't said a word, I've kept my mouth
             shut, because that's what I'm supposed to do. But if you
             want this account so bad I suggest you go down there
             and suck his dick. Because I'm not into that.

             (JO *leaves the office. Silence.*)

GAVIN   Pity.

             (*Loud disco music. Blackout.*)

Scene Five

*The office. The night of the party. Darkness outside. Down a corridor
the disco pulsates. The food is situated out of sight down the corridor
which leads to the disco. BOB and LEE enter. Both of them wear party
hats and are dressed up, but nothing too elaborate. BOB has a bottle of
red wine.*

BOB   Oh yes, oh yes.

LEE   Oh brilliant, eh?

BOB   Oh yes . . . I'm in tonight.

             (BOB *pours* LEE *a drink.*)

LEE   This looks like good stuff.

BOB   Oh yeh, Gav never skimps on the party. The cash flow
             might be shit, but the party's brill.

LEE   There's five Christmas parties going on tonight that I
             know of. If I don't pull I might leg it over to Patterson's.
             They reckon that's usually great.

             (BOB *tastes the wine.*)

BOB   Arh . . . fruity without being too permissive.

LEE	Hey you don't think we're going to lose anybody do you?
BOB	What with a hundred and eighty firms a day going bust? What do you think. We're all fucking doomed.
LEE	Yeh?
BOB	You are in tonight, mate.
LEE	Yeh?
BOB	Pippa. Oh yes. Begging for it.
LEE	You reckon?

(ANDY *enters from outside.*)

BOB	I thought you weren't coming.
ANDY	I did think about it. Get us a drink will you?
LEE	I'll get a glass.

(LEE *exits down the corridor.*)

BOB	They're going crazy in there already . . .
ANDY	Why do we do it?
BOB	You need a week off.
ANDY	I need the cash. Jenny's on about taking the kids out to another school now. She wants them to go private.
BOB	Where are they?
ANDY	Down at Millfield.
BOB	I wouldn't have let any of mine go there, it's full of drug addicts. They've got five year old junkies down there. They've got kids in pampers selling Ecstasy. Send the little sods private, do yourself a favour.

(LEE *returns with a glass and another bottle.*)

LEE	Reinforcements.
BOB	Good man.

ANDY	I don't believe in it.
	(ANDY *has a drink of wine.*)
BOB	Bloody kids. I wish we'd never had any. Wait till they get into their teens, that's when you'd wished you'd've shipped them off to Eton or somewhere.
	(GAVIN *enters, slightly oiled. He has been dancing.*)
GAVIN	Can't stand the pace, eh? Come on get back in there.
LEE	I can.
BOB	Andy's living in a fantasy, he still thinks there'll be a Labour government.
ANDY	I do.
GAVIN	There'll never be another Labour government, so you might as well get used to the idea.
ANDY	I'm pretty used to it already.
BOB	The kids are a bloody nightmare, there's computer discs and games all over the bloody house. All night they're playing with some stupid Sega game.
LEE	Have you seen the software for the new genie?
BOB	They bore me senseless.
ANDY	Bob's only interested in one thing.
GAVIN	Well a little bird told me that Patty's got a soft spot for you so I should watch it.
BOB	And if you believe that, you'll believe anything.
GAVIN	She's in there with Ted Payne.
BOB	I've forgotten what you do it's been so long.
ANDY	It's like riding a bike, you never forget.
GAVIN	Patty's a lovely woman.
BOB	She is.

GAVIN   And she's single.

ANDY   Is she?

GAVIN   You know he's left her?

ANDY   No, I didn't . . . Ohh . . .

BOB   Hey you're in Gav.

GAVIN   Yeh, I bet we'd all go the distance if we thought we
            could get away with it.

LEE   Get away with what?

GAVIN   Well maybe not Lee.

BOB   He's into software not underwear.

LEE   I'm not you know.

GAVIN   Yeh well, would an honest married man sleep with a
            beautiful woman if he knew that nobody would ever
            find out about it?

LEE   What, not even her?

GAVIN   What do you think, Andy?

ANDY   (*shaking his head*) Naaarrr . . .

BOB   There are no honest married men.

GAVIN   Bob?

BOB   And she's beautiful is she?

GAVIN   Bob, she's a bimbo.

BOB   Yes.

LEE   Actually I would.

GAVIN   You're not married.

LEE   No but I'm honest.

BOB .   Andy just think, no one would ever know about it.

ANDY	I know that.
BOB	Nobody would ever know about it. Ever.
LEE	You've got to get the woman to agree.
GAVIN	If the price is right . . .
BOB	Dead right, did you see that in the Telegraph? Did you see it? Some big city brokers firm had brought in a Strip-O-Gram, for one of the exec's birthdays. The next thing you know they were all having a go at her.
ANDY	Where was this?
BOB	It was in the bloody paper. They get strippers in and shag 'em during lunch. I think it's a good idea. Better than playing on the computer.
LEE	I'd have to agree there.
BOB	A cleaner caught one of them sat aside the MD. There you go Gav.
ANDY	When was this?
BOB	Last week.
LEE	It didn't give any phone numbers did it? (*They all laugh.*)
ANDY	Is it warm in here?
LEE	If you're warm in here, I'd keep out of there, it's like a sauna. You'll probably have a fit.
BOB	Hey be careful Lee, remember where you are.
LEE	Don't forget Bob, those you stand on on the way to the top, you meet on the way back down again.
GAVIN	I hope that's not true.
LEE	Well that's what my mother says.
BOB	Bless her.
LEE	Well, really, she's not my mother in reality.

BOB   Oh, she's a virtual mother is she?

             (*All laugh.*)

LEE   No. She's er . . .

BOB   Sorry, Lee.

LEE   It's just that I've still got all my computer stuff at my
             Gran's but I call her my mother.

BOB   Sounds more complicated than my life. Talk about
             spinning plates? I come to work, spin plates, go home,
             spin plates, she shouts, the kids cry, and I spin plates. I
             go to bed, can't sleep, and in the morning we're as right
             as rain, for nearly an hour. Now that's a happy marriage.
             There's only one problem.

LEE   You're dizzy from all that spinning?

BOB   I married the wrong fucking woman.

             (PIPPA *enters from the disco. She is clearly having a
             great time.*)

PIPPA   What're you doing? Come on, Gavin are you coming
             back or what? Bob? Andy? It's great in here, come on
             you farts . . . come and have a look at Patty, she's out
             of it. I think it must be her tranquillizers. Come on you
             boring old sods. Andy?

ANDY   Later, honest.

PIPPA   Honest?

ANDY   Yeh.

PIPPA   Oh you're boring. Bob come on . . .

             (PIPPA *exits.*)

BOB   (*to* LEE) I'm in there.

LEE   I thought it was me.

BOB   I'm telling you. Oh brilliant.

             (BOB *exits.*)

GAVIN	So how's Jenny?
ANDY	Fine, yeh, nearly finished the book, thank God. I've seen so little of her recently I was beginning to forget what she looked like.
GAVIN	I've always liked Jen.
ANDY	She's great.
GAVIN	Sorry about the late nights, mate.
ANDY	No problem.
GAVIN	My name must be dirt.
ANDY	Well, yes.
GAVIN	How's she feel about you working with a super-model!
ANDY	Eh?
GAVIN	I bet they'd get on. Have they met?
ANDY	Well actually . . .
GAVIN	Mind you, Jenny's broad-minded though, isn't she?
ANDY	How do you mean?
GAVIN	She's always struck me as broad-minded.
LEE	What did she say when she found out Jo wasn't a man? Same as us, eh? Bloody surprised I'll bet?
ANDY	Well actually, I haven't . . .
LEE	What she doesn't know about, eh?
ANDY	It's not that.
GAVIN	(*scoring a point*) Ah . . . I see.
ANDY	It's not . . .
GAVIN	. . . yes, I see.
ANDY	Hey listen . . .

LEE	Say no more . . .
GAVIN	He's covering aren't you?
ANDY	There's nothing to cover.
GAVIN	I see.
LEE	Oh right?
GAVIN	Airier . . .
ANDY	Oh come on!
GAVIN	Say no more squire.
ANDY	The fact that I haven't told her doesn't . . .
GAVIN	He's wriggling . . .
ANDY	I'll go and phone her now. Shall I? Just to make you all feel happy.
LEE	There's a phone there.
ANDY	What is this?
GAVIN	Nothing to do with us.
LEE	I'll do it if you like.
ANDY	Oh come on.
GAVIN	We know why you haven't.
ANDY	Here we go.
GAVIN	You and Jo, eh?
ANDY	Oh is that it?
GAVIN	Eh?
ANDY	Oh come on.
GAVIN	Oh look at him . . .
ANDY	What do you want me to say?
LEE	He's that 'right on' he's dropping off.
ANDY	She's just not my type.

GAVIN	No? I bet you'd like to . . .
LEE	Arrrrr . . .
ANDY	Oh come on.
GAVIN	What?
LEE	I would . . .
GAVIN	Admit it.
ANDY	No.
LEE	Admit it.
ANDY	You're a mile out.
LEE	I admit it.
GAVIN	Admit it.
ANDY	Why?
GAVIN	Admit it.
ANDY	No way.
LEE	Course you would. He'd probably like to tie her up and shag her stupid.
ANDY	(*angrily*) I'm not like them twats in the Telegraph, don't worry about that.
LEE	Get off man, we'd all like to, eh Gavin?
GAVIN	Not me.
LEE	Oh yeh, right.
GAVIN	What was that about tying her up?
LEE	Oh, what a giveaway.
	(BOB *enters with* PIPPA.)
BOB	Hey hey. She's got a tattoo on her arse! I'm gonna get a photocopy of it . . .
PIPPA	Look at me, I must be stupid.

LEE	Don't waste paper, remember.
PIPPA	I'm pissed up. I am.
BOB	Come on . . .

(BOB *exits towards the photocopying area with* PIPPA.)

LEE	How old is that man?
ANDY	Forty.
LEE	He's running around like a fifty year old.
ANDY	For a change.
GAVIN	I hope he dies . . . (*Laughs at himself.*) No. Sorry.

(PATTY *enters with a plate of food. She is quite high. She is singing "It's Raining Men", by the Weather Girls. She places the food on a desk and begins to move to the music.*)

ANDY	Patty?
GAVIN	Bob's looking for you, Pat.
PATTY	There'll be none left soon, so if you don't get some now you've had it.
GAVIN	What would we do without you?
PATTY	All the chicken's gone, there's two sausages left, and there's mousse all over the floor. Come on get moving . . . (*She begins to sing, and dance, very badly.*) "I'm gonna go out, I'm gonna let myself get . . . absolutely soaking wet" . . . (PATTY *is dancing, oblivious to the others.*) Oh come on Andy! Get into it . . .
ANDY	Oh Patty . . .
PATTY	Come on . . .

(ANDY *begins to dance, very badly.*)

"Hallelujah, it's raining men, Amen." Get into it Gav, you stiff old sod.

ANDY	What are you doing?
PATTY	"North, south, east, west I'm gonna let myself get soaking wet."
LEE	Is she drunk?
ANDY	(*laughing*) She's either drunk or mad.
GAVIN	I love it . . .

(GAVIN *starts to dance. He is clearly quite drunk and slips and staggers slightly.* LEE *also begins to dance.* BOB *enters with* PIPPA. *He has a photocopy of a butterfly. On a buttock.*)

BOB	Oh yes look at this.
PIPPA	God, I'm gonna die.

(BOB *attaches the image to a wall.*)

BOB	And she's got a wicked side to her, she nearly had me in there.
PIPPA	Don't be daft. I didn't.
BOB	You should've seen her.
PIPPA	I couldn't get on the machine, I got my leg stuck. He kept looking.
BOB	I didn't.
GAVIN	I think I've seen that butterfly somewhere before.
PIPPA	Bob says he can tell my personality from that.
BOB	Definitely an extrovert.
GAVIN	Go on Patty, you're next . . .
PATTY	(*still dancing*) I love this.

BOB	And then as if by magic. (BOB *reveals another photocopy, this time of his own bottom.*) Da dar . . . Bob Marsden's 'Ring Cycle'.

(*There is a big cheer, as* BOB *displays the photocopy of his rear.*)

ANDY	It's his face . . .
LEE	Put some glasses on it.
GAVIN	It's an improvement Bob.
BOB	I'm gonna fax this to some bastard, what do you think, Andy? The ultimate arse.

(BOB *and* PIPPA *exit.*)

PATTY	I love this . . . Girls just want to have fun. Come on every . . . Oh Christmas, I love it.
GAVIN	What's she on?
LEE	Another planet.
PATTY	(*grabbing* LEE) I could eat you . . .
LEE	Yeh? I'm at the peak of my sexual powers, you know.
PATTY	So am I!

(*They all begin to dance. All of them equally embarrassing. It is funny and surreal. During this,* JO *enters. She looks very sexy in a short, but low-cut black dress. She surveys this scene from the steps. She is slightly tipsy herself and stumbles ever so slightly on the staircase.*)

LEE	Hey look out . . . get the rope out Andy.
ANDY	Very good . . .
GAVIN	Come on.
LEE	Have you been tied up Jo?
JO	Sorry?

LEE   You would be.

PATTY   "Coz girls just want to have fun, that's all they want . . .
           just want to have fun . . ."

GAVIN   Get her a drink!

PATTY   That's all they waaaaant . . .

ANDY   Is it warm in here?

PATTY   Yes girls just want to have fun.

GAVIN   Merry Christmas Andy.

ANDY   Yeh right.

           (BOB *enters with* PIPPA. *He is gleeful.*)

BOB   Hey guess what! I've just faxed my fucking arse to
           Patterson's . . .

           (BOB *laughs uproariously. The music swells. All dance
           save* JO *who surveys this anarchy from the staircase.
           Slow curtain as they all dance.*)

ACT TWO

Scene One

The office. Much later, almost midnight. As the characters emerge from the disco we see them in various stages of "relaxation". Ties are cast aside, shirt-tails are out, and the heat of the disco means sweat stains appear on some of the men. The curtains rises and we see that this area of the office is now quite a mess. The disco still pulsates down the corridor. ANDY *is on stage, he is more dishevelled than earlier. He is getting some air near a window, and he is clearly well-oiled. He grabs a glass of wine, and knocks it back. He looks at his watch.* PIPPA, *who by now is having the time of her life, comes from the disco.*

PIPPA   You're a dark horse!

ANDY   Am I?

PIPPA   Ohhh . . .

ANDY   There you go.

PIPPA   Yeh.

ANDY   Yeh, when I've had a drink I'm anybody's.

PIPPA   I know what you mean.

ANDY   Mis-spent youth.

PIPPA   Not a bad dancer, are you?

ANDY   Aren't I?

PIPPA   You're good.

ANDY   Am I?

PIPPA   Where did you learn to dance like that?

ANDY   Like what?

PIPPA   All that floppy stuff.

ANDY   That's with my nerves.

PIPPA   Oh yeh, what's it called?

ANDY	The Office Flop.
PIPPA	Really?
ANDY	Yeh.
PIPPA	It could catch on.
ANDY	It already has. There are thousands of office workers all over the world who can only dance the Flop.
PIPPA	You're joking?
ANDY	Oh dear . . .
PIPPA	And have you seen Jo?
ANDY	Well . . .
PIPPA	Bloody hell, who's does she think she is, Madonna?
ANDY	Yeh, she's going for it isn't she?
	(PIPPA *goes to look at her butterfly which is still blue-tacked to the wall.*)
PIPPA	Phew, hot isn't it?
ANDY	It is in there . . .
PIPPA	I'm boiled.
ANDY	You're all over the place.
PIPPA	I'm all right.
ANDY	You're not driving are you?
PIPPA	That's my bum.
ANDY	I know.
PIPPA	(*looking at the photocopy*) Gooor, isn't it weird? Do you think it looks like me?
ANDY	(*considers the image and* PIPPA'S *rear*) Well . . .
PIPPA	I don't think that looks like mine.

ANDY	Why did you have it done?
PIPPA	Dunno. I was going to have one on my arm, but I thought that was a bit boring. It is a bit boring really, isn't it?
ANDY	I suppose.
PIPPA	A bit boring really.
ANDY	Well . . .
PIPPA	Have you got any tattoos?
ANDY	Yeh I've got 'coward' tattooed down the middle of my back.
PIPPA	Have you?
ANDY	I feel as if I have.
PIPPA	Have you?
ANDY	What are you going to feel like tomorrow?
PIPPA	Sod tomorrow. That's my motto.
ANDY	That was mine twenty years ago.
PIPPA	Are you coming back?
ANDY	Ohhh . . . do I have to?
PIPPA	Come on you coward, what are you scared of?
ANDY	You. That Ingrid . . .
PIPPA	And we all know about her.
ANDY	The tall woman from Market Research.
PIPPA	Come on . . .

(PIPPA *almost drags* ANDY *towards the entrance of the disco. As they make their way* PATTY *comes from the disco. She has a bottle of wine and a glass, she is still quite a bit out of it. She appears to be still quite high, she sings.*)

PATTY   "The only way is up, baby, for you and me now, the
only way is up . . . that's the only way, up go
up it's the only way . . . up up up . . . oh yeh, hold on . . ."

PIPPA   (*joining in*) "Hold on . . ."

PATTY   Oooohh . . .

PIPPA   "Hold on . . ."

ANDY   Oh bloody hell . . .

PATTY   Hold on, the only way is up, Andy!

ANDY   So they say.

PIPPA   Isn't he lovely, eh? Don't you think? Isn't he sweet?
He's the best bloke in the office, aren't you?

ANDY   You're only saying that because it's true.

PIPPA   I'm not.

ANDY   You should be.

PATTY   Looks like you're in.

ANDY   I'm in everywhere tonight, so they tell me.

PIPPA   I love her.

ANDY   Do you?

PIPPA   I love you . . .

(PIPPA *gives* PATTY *a hug. It's a drunken, awkward,
over-emotional hug.* PATTY *has to respond.* ANDY *laughs
awkwardly.*)

PATTY   You have a good night, eh . . .

PIPPA   I love her . . .

ANDY   Well you won't need me then will you?

PIPPA   Come on . . .

(PIPPA *takes* ANDY *off stage into the disco.* PATTY *makes
her way over to the food table. She helps herself to a*

few scraps of food. She then sits quite deliberately on a
swivel chair and spins herself around. As she spins, Jo
enters from the disco. She too has been dancing and has
come for a breather.)

JO   Safety, at last!

PATTY   That's right.

JO   Ken West.

PATTY   Desperate Ken.

JO   He dances like a crab.

PATTY   I know.

JO   We were nearly out in the canal.

PATTY   I've just had Ted Payne all over me like a rash.

JO   Oh lucky you.

PATTY   Sad bastard.

JO   There's two girls from Production who are topless.

PATTY   I saw that coming.

JO   What are they playing at?

PATTY   Christmas, eh?

JO   Sad.

PATTY   I quite like it.

JO   How do you feel?

PATTY   I ought to know better.

JO   Well . . .

PATTY   I shouldn't really dance.

JO   Have you seen Bob?

PATTY   You can't miss him.

JO   What's he playing at?

PATTY	He's always like that.
JO	He's spread mousse all over his chest . . .
PATTY	Well at least he's still got his clothes on.
JO	Just.
PATTY	There's time.
JO	I don't think I've ever seen so many bad dancers.
PATTY	I have.
JO	Yeh?
PATTY	I worked in insurance before I came here . . . Whoooo.
JO	Constipated?
JO	Frightening.
PATTY	I bet.
JO	Their Christmas party looked like martians had landed. Now that was sad. All year these poor little suits would sit and say nothing, and then for five hours at Christmas they went crazy. I think some of them actually died from alcohol abuse. Come the new year they were back behind their desks.
JO	Back to reality.
PATTY	Why do we do it?
JO	All part of the job, isn't it?
PATTY	I mean look at Bob! Every year he looks forward to this, and the most he can hope for is a tongue job.
JO	Urrrgh.
PATTY	I don't know about you, but I would have to be very, very desperate to slip into reprographics with Bob.
JO	Well I think he's got his eye on you.
PATTY	No it's you.

Jo	Oh yeh?
Patty	You're the new girl. You're this year's catch. Didn't you know?
Jo	Funny, I hadn't realised.
Patty	You're Cinderella this year. Take my advice, cling on to Andy before Gav moves in.
Jo	Right.
Patty	He's on the hunt.
Jo	I hadn't noticed.
Patty	Oh yes . . .
Jo	It's ok, I'll just nut him . . .
Patty	Oh yeh?
Jo	Wouldn't that be great?
Patty	For you maybe.
Jo	That'd solve a lot of problems.
Patty	Men aren't after me that much Jo, I can't afford to be nutting them.
Jo	He's another one who comes on a bit.
Patty	Not all the time.
Jo	Oh, what does that mean?
Patty	Arrggh . . .
Jo	Arrggh what?
Patty	Oh yes . . .
Jo	Sounds like you're speaking from experience?
Patty	I am.
Jo	Oh right.
Patty	Oh yes I am.

Jo	What?
Patty	Arrggh.
Jo	I see.
Patty	Yeh.
Jo .	Ah.
Patty	Oh yes.
Jo	I thought you were a shy mother of two?
Patty	No, I'm a sad mother of two.
Jo	Doesn't sound like it.
Patty	Ah ah . . . Yeh, well. Now you know. You're not the only one with a life of glamour.
Jo	I never thought I was.
Patty	Good old Gavin.
Jo	So did he try it on?
Patty	Not really.
Jo	Oh.
Patty	I did.
Jo	Eh?
Patty	Yeh.
Jo	Patty!
Patty	Yeh. Shy old, boring old me.
Jo	Bloody hell.
Patty	Ych. Tired of being the victim, I went for it.
Jo	And?
Patty	What?
Jo	Go on then.

PATTY	Nothing.
JO	What?
PATTY	Absolutely nothing.
JO	I don't believe you.
PATTY	Yeh.
JO	What, he couldn't?
PATTY	No.
JO	Was it you?
PATTY	No . . .
JO	When was this?
PATTY	Birmingham, Hyatt.
JO	So . . .
PATTY	He wouldn't. He was all for it downstairs. Then I got to my room, got it all nicely worked out, and when we got into bed he wouldn't.
JO	Gavin?
PATTY	He wouldn't touch me. Suddenly, woooff, switch off.
	(*Silence.*)
	That's sad. Isn't it? Don't you think? That's what sad is. "Sad" is getting to the juicy stuff and suddenly nothing. So we just slept together. It was ok actually, at least it wasn't violent, that made a change. (*Lighter.*) Oh, eh?
JO	He was probably . . .
PATTY	He just didn't want me. He kept saying I was too nice. I wasn't too nice, I was too old, that's what he meant. My battle plan didn't work out. I'd got him back to my camp but I surrendered too soon. I've never been any good at all that.
JO	Well you must be doing something right.

PATTY   How come?

JO   Two kids.

PATTY   It's the games. I can't play the games.

JO   Neither can I.

PATTY   Oh yes you can.

JO   No, I can't. I was engaged and married to Neil before I realised he fancied me.

PATTY   Oh yeh?

JO   That's the truth. He kept buying me flowers. I'd never had that before. I thought, "this is a bit weird." And the next thing you know . . .

PATTY   The perfect marriage!

JO   That's right.

PATTY   And he trusts you and you trust him?

JO   That's right.

PATTY   All alone in the frozen north! With the likes of Ken West running loose. Where men are men and sheep are frightened?

JO   If I know that lot they'll be rubbing mousse into their nipples as well. They're big on bonding in the city.

PATTY   Bonding or bondage?

JO   Probably both.

PATTY   Parties eh? Great fun. (*Ironic.*) I'm loving it. I've got two kids and a husband who left me for a little tart. Ho, ho, ho, children — Merry Christmas.

         (PATTY *stands and is about to leave for the disco, when* LEE *enters with a fax. He is laughing excitedly.*)

LEE   Look at this.

JO   There you go Patty, just what you're looking for.

PATTY   A toy boy . . .

LEE   That's me.

PATTY   You're not faxing bits of yourself all over Leeds, are
            you?

LEE   This is brilliant.

            (*As* LEE *reads the details of the fax,* BOB *enters. His shirt
            is wide open and his large pale frame hangs from his
            shoulders. He is having a great time. He shows off with
            a little dance.*)

BOB   Here he is, the disco king. (*Sings.*) "Burn baby burn, it's
            a disco inferno . . . burn baby burn."

PATTY   Pass me the sick bag.

JO   Very nice Bob, very, very stylish.

BOB   What about that for a body?

JO   What can I say?

BOB   I could advertise fucking anything with this body.

LEE   Hey Bob, your arse's come back.

BOB   What?

LEE   Patterson's have faxed your arse back.

BOB   What?

LEE   Yeh.

BOB   Cheeky bastards.

LEE   And they made some notes for improvement.

BOB   What?

LEE   Suggested alterations, it says.

BOB   That arse is perfect.

LEE   They think it's too hairy.

BOB	No way.
LEE	They don't think there's a market for it.
BOB	Cheeky sods.
JO	It's a cruel world Bob. It must be awful to be told that our bum is just not up to scratch.
BOB	I'll fax 'em my wedding tackle in a minute.
LEE	Good idea.
BOB	I don't need 'em anyway.
JO	Remember we're trying to do business with them?
BOB	Why don't you fax 'em yours? I bet they wouldn't send that back.
JO	Oh, I don't know.
BOB	Not from what I've heard about you and Patterson.
JO	Ha, ha!
BOB	Hey be a sport, get on the photocopier!
JO	Not tonight.
BOB	Yeh come on, I'll do you an arse reading.
	(BOB *laughs at his audaciousness.*)
JO	You're wasted here, Bob.
BOB	I fucking know that.
LEE	You're not going home yet are you?
JO	I'm only just getting warmed up.
LEE	Oh brilliant. I've got to get my Christmas kisses yet.
JO	I thought you were after Pippa?
BOB	He is, he's in there but he just doesn't know how to play it.
JO	Unlike you, eh?

(PATTY *makes her way back into the disco*.)

PATTY   Oh, oh listen. I love this . . . Oh Motown, bloody hell Motown. This takes me back. The good old days . . .

BOB   Patty, I'll be back in a minute.

PATTY   Name that tune? Martha Reeves and the Vandellas!

(PATTY *has left the office*.)

BOB   I'm in there!

LEE   I thought you were in with Pippa?

BOB   No that's you!

LEE   You said you were 'in' with Ingrid?

BOB   I am in there, no trouble.

LEE   Yeh?

BOB   I bet my mortgage. I'll move in when we do the Conga.

(LEE *is still considering the fax*.)

LEE   You know, I don't believe somebody would actually do this.

BOB   Cheeky sods!

LEE   Back to the drawing board.

BOB   I mean that is my bum they're talking about.

LEE   Somebody has actually received this fax, and spent a good half hour making copious notes about it. That can only mean one thing.

BOB   What?

LEE   Well, Patterson's party is either deathly boring or whoever did this is a true professional.

BOB   Absolutely right.

LEE	And it's reassuring to know that we are dealing with professionals here.
BOB	Right I'm back in there . . . has all the red gone?
	(BOB *searches through empty bottles*.)
LEE	There's some lager in Gav's office.
BOB	Saving it for himself, crafty sod.
	(BOB *staggers towards the disco*.)
	Whoops!
LEE	I think you've had it.
BOB	No way. I've done a bit of tactical stuff. Ignore 'em for the first two hours and then full frontal attack.
	(BOB *makes his way to the disco room. He turns and does a little dance. As* BOB *disappears,* PIPPA *comes back into the office. She looks through the empty bottles*.)
PIPPA	Andy wants a drink.
LEE	There's no red left.
PIPPA	Oh.
LEE	Good party, eh?
PIPPA	Yeh.
LEE	I don't know about you but I'm as pissed as a fart.
PIPPA	Well blow away then.
LEE	Eh?
PIPPA	Joke.
LEE	They reckon there's going to be redundancies.
PIPPA	That's because of you and Bob wasting paper.
LEE	It isn't.
PIPPA	I bet it is.

LEE	I work my balls off here.
PIPPA	Well you're no good to me then.
LEE	Ah, sod it. If I get dropped I'll just stay in bed and play with my computer.
PIPPA	Play with your what?
LEE	Have you got any hobbies?
PIPPA	Yeh, I sing.
LEE	You never.
PIPPA	I do. In a choir.
LEE	You never.
PIPPA	Yeh, yeh I do.
LEE	You never.
PIPPA	No, no I never.
LEE	Arrggh . . . I thought so.
	(*Pause.*)
	Where do you live then?
PIPPA	Why?
LEE	Well . . .
PIPPA	Are you trying to chat me up?
LEE	Maybe.
PIPPA	Well are you or aren't you?
LEE	Yeh I am, yeh.
PIPPA	Oh right.
LEE	Yeh I am.
PIPPA	I thought so.
	(*Pause.*)
LEE	Yeh, yeh I am.

PIPPA	Go on then.
LEE	Gavin calls me Nero sometimes.
PIPPA	Oh yeh.
LEE	He says I'm always fiddling about.
PIPPA	Oh right.
LEE	I call him Gavin.
PIPPA	We all do.
LEE	Did you know that Bob knows where every Little Chef is located in Great Britain?
PIPPA	No.
LEE	Whenever he's on a long journey he stops at the Little Chef.
PIPPA	Oh right.
LEE	He told me.
PIPPA	Oh, that's interesting.
LEE	He has the all-day breakfast . . .
PIPPA	Right.
LEE	You know, bacon, sausage, egg, fried bread . . .
PIPPA	I'm not thick.
	(*Silence.*)
LEE	Great party.
	(*Silence.* LEE *begins to move to the music. He is quite simply an awful dancer.* PIPPA *cannot believe he is quite so bad, and can hardly hide her sniggers.*)
	I'm not much of a party animal.
PIPPA	Really?
	(*Silence.*)
LEE	So what sort of car are you driving at the moment?

PIPPA   Why, you're not coming in it!

LEE   (*has to laugh his way out of it*) Oh yeh, nice one.

             (ANDY *comes in from the disco. He is sweating heavily.*)

ANDY   Oh thanks, I'm gagging in there!

PIPPA   Eh?

ANDY   Where's my drink?

PIPPA   Sorry.

ANDY   Can't trust you, can I? You promise me the earth, you
             promise me a wonderful relationship, and you forget my
             drink.

PIPPA   Lee's been telling me about Bob's eating habits.

ANDY   Oh dear. (*He reclines in a chair.*) I must be getting old.

LEE   Bob's arse came back.

ANDY   So I hear.

PIPPA   Are we going back in then or what?

LEE   Who me?

PIPPA   Are you coming?

ANDY   No that's it for me. I've flopped enough for tonight.

PIPPA   Ohhh.

             (PIPPA *makes her way towards the disco.* LEE *is left with*
             ANDY.)

ANDY   Aren't you going in?

LEE   Dunno.

ANDY   What's wrong?

LEE   It's me, I'm shit at the chat up. I actually asked her what
             sort of car she was driving.

ANDY   Oh.

LEE	How pathetic.
ANDY	What is she driving?
	(*A beat.*)
LEE	Didn't say.
ANDY	I think she comes on the bus anyway.
LEE	I can't do it, I'm doomed. I can't think of what to say.
ANDY	You should've drawn her a picture.
LEE	I just can't talk to 'em.
ANDY	Well if you go in there you're well away — nobody can hear a word you say anyway.
	(BOB *enters from the disco, looking wilder and wilder. He is searching for some food amongst the plates* PATTY *brought in.*)
BOB	Well that's it then.
LEE	What?
BOB	All the food's gone.
LEE	I've only had a chicken leg.
BOB	Tough.
LEE	I'm starving.
BOB	Well if you want something else you'll have to eat somebody.
LEE	What happened to the full-frontal assault?
BOB	Ted Payne's moved in, anyway there's time yet. Isn't that right Andy?
ANDY	What's that?
BOB	Plenty of time yet?
ANDY	Oh yes.

BOB	Ohhh, yes.
ANDY	What?
BOB	Lucky bastard. Give her one for me will you?
ANDY	Oh Bob . . .
BOB	Nice mouth, eh? Don't you think Lee, nice mouth?
LEE	Who?
BOB	Oh yes.
ANDY	What are you doing out here Bob? You're wasting valuable time.
BOB	So are you.
ANDY	That's right.
BOB	I'll tell you this, if I don't shag somebody tonight, there is no justice. I am working my bollocks off in there. I haven't worked so hard since the 'freshers ball.' Look at me, I bet I've lost a stone?
LEE	Keep up the good work, Bob.
BOB	But he is well in, aren't you?
ANDY	Am I?
BOB	Oh come on?
ANDY	You've got me all wrong, Bob.
BOB	Have I bollocks.
ANDY	No?
BOB	The trouble with you is, you're too concerned what people think about you. Look at me. I don't give a toss what people think about me.
ANDY	We know that.
BOB	Relax, man.
ANDY	Yeh?

BOB   You tosser!

ANDY   Yeh?

BOB   That's what you are, a tosser.

ANDY   That's right.

BOB   When I was at college I used to piss on people like you.
           I mean literally. Toss-bags. Too many problems up here.
           (*His head.*) Don't give me the moral maze, you tosser.

ANDY   Anyway Bob, thanks . . .

BOB   I know the world's in chaos Andy, one sly little fuck
           won't hurt, you know?

ANDY   What's that got to do with it?

BOB   Relax, have one night off, let yourself fucking go.

ANDY   Like you?

BOB   Ok, I have the odd fuck-bag in Brussels or Amsterdam,
           but it's not the end of the world, is it?

LEE   You what?

BOB   And it's legal there, I'm not breaking any rules am I?
           When in Holland live as the Dutch, that's the way I see
           it.

LEE   Where's all this come from?

BOB   But that's your problem isn't it?

ANDY   What?

BOB   You think that if you're unfaithful to Jenny the entire
           fabric of western civilisation will crumble. Come on,
           she's been stuck in a bedroom writing a kids book for
           the past two years. I bet you hardly see her. She's there
           writing about Binky Ben and the Nobbly Knoll, and
           you're here sweating like a twat because Jo's dancing
           with everybody except you. I'm not thick, you know?
           I mean listen, it's Christmas, forget Jenny and the kids,

forget your mother — she's dead anyway. She won't say anything about it.

ANDY   Thanks Bob.

BOB   Just do it for yourself, get in there and snog her or something. Do something.

ANDY   Have another drink, Bob.

BOB   Don't be a wimp all your life Andy, get in there and show us what your made of.

ANDY   You're priceless, did you know that?

BOB   I'm not frightened of the world, like you. I'll tell you that. If you don't move in here tonight you'll regret it for the rest of your life.

ANDY   Anyway Bob . . .

BOB   I can't waste my time out here with you tossers.

          (BOB *turns to exit.* GAVIN *enters.*)

GAVIN   Bobby boy . . .

BOB   Gavin . . . can I say tossers?

GAVIN   What?

BOB   Can I say tossers?

GAVIN   You can.

BOB   Andy. A very very disappointing show. I'm in there.

          (BOB *makes his way towards the disco.* ANDY *is relieved* BOB *has left.* GAVIN *settles himself. He is drunk and sweating heavily.*)

GAVIN   All right, Nero?

LEE   Yeh brilliant.

GAVIN   You pulled yet?

LEE   Nearly, just putting the final touches to it.

GAVIN	Good man.
LEE	Well you know, some of us have got it.
GAVIN	Get in there mate.
LEE	I'm just going.
GAVIN	The DJ's shit, but you can't have everything can you?
LEE	You have.

(LEE *laughs at himself. He makes his way towards the disco, clearly feeling a little deflated. He goes to look for a drink. He gets the last dregs out of a bottle of white wine.*)

GAVIN	Ooohh it's still there Andy, I've still got it.
ANDY	Oh yeh?
GAVIN	Still got the touch.
ANDY	I had it, then I lost it. It must have flopped out.
GAVIN	Have you seen those two with their tops off? What are they playing at?
ANDY	Woodstock.
GAVIN	Who are they trying to shock?
ANDY	Not you.
GAVIN	That's right.
ANDY	You're unshockable.
GAVIN	That's right.
ANDY	Yeh.
GAVIN	But what do you do? They work hard, so they deserve to let their hair down. I dunno, I'm going to have to have a word with Ted Payne, I mean his whole department are going crazy. I'm going to have to report him. (*He laughs at his own joke.*)
ANDY	Very good.

GAVIN   Arrggh.

ANDY   Very good.

             (GAVIN *sits and relaxes*.)

GAVIN   Getting old, mate. I can't keep up with some of that lot.

ANDY   Yeh, Pippa ought to take a battery out.

GAVIN   Can you imagine it with her?

ANDY   Oh dear . . .

GAVIN   I think she's on acid.

ANDY   She's on something.

GAVIN   Getting old.

ANDY   Oh dear.

             (*A beat*.)

GAVIN   Mind you . . .

ANDY   What?

GAVIN   You're in.

ANDY   Don't. I've just had Bob.

GAVIN   Arrggh?

ANDY   What?

GAVIN   Arrggh . . . ?

ANDY   No.

GAVIN   Arrggh . . . ?

ANDY   What can you do?

GAVIN   Not my type, you said.

ANDY   I did.

GAVIN   We got your number didn't we?

ANDY   Bloody Christmas!

GAVIN	Oh dear. Old age mate.
ANDY	Oh dear.
GAVIN	We got your number.
ANDY	Yeh.
GAVIN	I like her.
ANDY	She's great.
GAVIN	She is.
ANDY	She is.
GAVIN	She is great. But what can you do?
ANDY	Very little.
GAVIN	She's great, and you're married.
ANDY	Oh dear.
GAVIN	And she can move, eh?
ANDY	Oh yes . . .
GAVIN	Oh yes.
ANDY	Took me back.
GAVIN	Straight in there. Wooosh. She's dancin' and you are in there.
ANDY	One dance.
GAVIN	In there . . .
ANDY	She's dancin' with everybody, Gavin.
GAVIN	Poor Jenny?
ANDY	It's just a . . .
GAVIN	And I'll tell you this, she likes to talk dirty.
ANDY	Oh yeh?
GAVIN	Oh yes.

ANDY   Oh.

GAVIN   Her and Patterson.

ANDY   You reckon?

GAVIN   Something.

ANDY   Oh dear.

            (GAVIN *makes his way to a chair, stumbles slightly, and lands himself neatly on a desk.*)

GAVIN   Oh well.

ANDY   Oh God.

GAVIN   I'm a bit disappointed actually.

ANDY   Oh yeh?

GAVIN   I thought I might be in with a shout, but . . .

ANDY   You never know.

GAVIN   No way. Ah, eh? Pity Caroline's not here.

ANDY   Are you joking?

GAVIN   Oh God.

ANDY   Well . . .

GAVIN   I miss her, you know?

            (GAVIN *laughs, then remembers.*)

            Thirteen years and she runs off with a little shite like that. Eh? What a little shit!

ANDY   Well, live and let live.

GAVIN   And I thought he was a queer!

ANDY   Shit happens . . .

GAVIN   I thought, well there's no danger there, he plays for the other team. And then, whoosh, she's off.

ANDY	You never know.
GAVIN	Off like that.
ANDY	Well?
GAVIN	I thought he was a queer.
ANDY	And now you know.
GAVIN	How wrong.
ANDY	Absolutely. Yes.
GAVIN	I am seldom wrong about people, but . . . there you go.
ANDY	There you go.
GAVIN	I knew there was something going on. She was being nice to me all the time. A year. Can you believe it? A year.
ANDY	Maybe she'll come back?
GAVIN	No, no she won't. There's just one thing I hope for.
ANDY	What's that?
GAVIN	That she doesn't make a go of it.
ANDY	I heard she was pitching for Patterson's?
GAVIN	That's right.
ANDY	Well you beat her there.
GAVIN	Yes but it's not sorted, is it?
ANDY	I thought . . .
GAVIN	Jo's dropped a bollock, hasn't she?
ANDY	Well I heard . . .
GAVIN	Arh, yes.
ANDY	I didn't ask you know?
GAVIN	Very good.

ANDY   I didn't feel. I only heard. Sounded a bit?

GAVIN   Sounded a bit dodgy. Now we might be up shit creek.

ANDY   I heard he came on a bit . . .

GAVIN   Did he come on or did she come on?

ANDY   That is the question?

GAVIN   She told me he got his old man out for her.

ANDY   Yeh, I heard.

GAVIN   Just whipped it out. Whooof, bang-out.

ANDY   That's not on, is it?

GAVIN   Told you she liked to talk dirty.

ANDY   That's not on.

GAVIN   That is definitely not on.

ANDY   That's right.

GAVIN   I told her. I said, "That is not on. That is definitely not
            on. No way is that on." But what can I do?

ANDY   Well . . .

GAVIN   He got it out, she said "no" and now he's saying "no".
            He's on about taking the account somewhere else.

ANDY   To Caroline?

GAVIN   And what I want to do is say to Patterson you are well
            out of order.

ANDY   That's right.

GAVIN   I want to support her.

ANDY   That's right.

GAVIN   But what can I do?

ANDY   You should support her.

GAVIN   I know.

ANDY   That's right.

GAVIN   But I can't rip the strip off him can I? Because what will he say?

ANDY   Stuff it!

GAVIN   Stuff it, exactly.

ANDY   Arrggh.

GAVIN   So we wait. And I'll go with an olive branch.

ANDY   Good idea.

GAVIN   And a big stick. Because we could do with that one.

ANDY   That's right.

GAVIN   Everybody's worked hard. You've worked hard. Bloody hell, late nights, Jenny going crazy, probably. Doing her nut and you lying to her, and we don't get it? Waste.

ANDY   That's right.

GAVIN   Oh, but you know?

ANDY   What?

GAVIN   Something.

ANDY   Yeh?

GAVIN   Must've played him on, though.

ANDY   Eh?

GAVIN   She must've gone a bit too far? 'Cos she's a bit touchy. Isn't she?

ANDY   Well I mean she's . . .

GAVIN   Yeh.

ANDY   No.

GAVIN   Of course she did.

ANDY   I can't see it . . .

GAVIN   She must've given him a fancy nod or something.

ANDY   You reckon?

GAVIN   Oh, come on?

ANDY   Well . . .

GAVIN   She must have.

ANDY   She wouldn't.

GAVIN   She must have.

ANDY   Maybe?

GAVIN   I mean you don't just whip your gonads out for nothing
             do you?

ANDY   Well . . .

GAVIN   I mean you don't just plonk it on the dashboard unless
             she's given you the wink, do you?

ANDY   Well that hasn't been my experience, no.

GAVIN   Or maybe you do? Maybe that's where we've been
             going wrong Andy, we haven't been flashing our bits
             about. Well I haven't, I don't, how about you?

ANDY   Not recently.

GAVIN   But I mean come on. You can see what she's like. She
             led him on, didn't she?

ANDY   I can't see it.

GAVIN   Oh man. Yes. Yes, it's obvious. He's worth two million,
             she's had a drink, thinks she's in for a session, gives him
             the nod and bingo. It's so obvious. She was asking for it.

ANDY   I don't think . . .

GAVIN   Yeh, yeh, of course. It happens all the time. And I tell
             you this, it serves her fucking right.

*(A sudden explosion of music. The entire office staff
burst through from the disco. They are all doing the
Conga.* BOB *is outrageous, he is behind* PATTY, LEE *is
hanging onto* PIPPA, JO *is at the tail end of the Conga
but she is certainly having a good time.* GAVIN *stands
and joins in the Conga. He reels as he is extremely
drunk.* ANDY *stands and cheers the others. All begin
to dance wildly. They dance on tables, desks, chairs.*
GAVIN *is well out of control. It is an explosion of party!
Music swells, and the lights fade on an image of great
debauchery.)*

Scene Two

*Lights slowly rise. The office is covered with streamers and paper
plates.* GAVIN *sits centre in a swivel chair, and appears to be
completely out of it. The rest of the office have gone, the disco has
stopped and only these characters remain.* BOB *is exceptionally drunk,
and all of them have seen the heat of battle.* LEE *sits looking at a
WP.* PATTY *is ready to leave. Time has moved on, the twilight zone of
partyland. The atmosphere is far more relaxed, and the characters are
now pathetically worse for wear.* LEE *toots on a hooter.*

GAVIN   *(tired)* Goodnight . . . *(He is drifting.)*

PIPPA   Feel sick . . . Oughhhh . . . *(She exits.)*

JO   God it's so bloody hot/

ANDY   I'm melting.

JO   I'm burning up/

BOB   Do your arse Jo/

JO   Spin on it Bob. *(She exits.)*

PATTY   I've got to go. Everyone else has gone. Just us lot as
             usual.

GAVIN   Goodnight Pat, sleep tight Pat.

             *(*LEE *toots.)*

PATTY   Shit, look at the time!

BOB	Don't go yet Patty, we haven't had time to chat.
PATTY	Maybe next year Bob/
ANDY	Go on Patty, take him home . . .
BOB	Come on hey . . . come here you/
PATTY	Not tonight Bob, thanks. Maybe in another life.
BOB	But we haven't had time to talk have we?/
	(LEE *toots*.)
GAVIN	Goodnight.
PATTY	What have we got to talk about?
BOB	We should have a little chat. We can have a chat. Me and you eh, come on Patty. Tell me about the husband, eh?
PATTY	Let's leave it shall we?
BOB	I mean why did he leave you?
PATTY	Wouldn't you like to know?
BOB	You can tell me you know, because I know about marriage, you know. I'd never leave you Patty.
	(BOB *attempts to get to his feet*.)
	I'd never leave you, I'd worship you I would. Like you deserve to be worshipped.
PATTY	Oh Bob, you say the sweetest things . . .
BOB	I would.
PATTY	(*soft*) Would you?
BOB	I would. I would not abuse you or use you.
PATTY	I'm sure you would . . . yeh . . .
BOB	Here look . . . look at this. These are my kids.

(He produces a wallet and some photos. PATTY *briefly looks but it's the opportunity to get near to her that he's after. He slightly stumbles and grabs* PATTY.*)*

These are my kids. Look — ha ha ha, look. Kids are great, you know why, you can tell them absolutely anything and they believe you. (*He studies the photograph.*) That's France. Matthew and Holly. I bet you can't guess where that is . . . eh?

PATTY   It's France Bob, you've just said.

BOB   Yeh yeh . . . but where is it?

PATTY   I don't know.

BOB   Near Lille that . . . near Lille.

PATTY   I would never have guessed.

BOB   Ha . . . so you've learnt something. My family that.

PATTY   Oh right, nice . . .

BOB   (*pointing to himself in the picture*) That's me.

PATTY   Nice.

BOB   That's the wife.

PATTY   Yeh.

BOB   She's a bit fat . . . don't you think? She's a bit overweight my wife.

PATTY   Well she suits you Bob doesn't she?

BOB   She's a fat pig my wife, Patty. A fat swine.

PATTY   No she isn't, she looks nice . . .

BOB   Hey listen — listen, call me Bob.

PATTY   I am calling you Bob.

LEE   When the red-red-Robin goes Bob-Bob-Bobbin along . . .

BOB   I need to talk to you . . .

ANDY	Haaaa . . . go on, Bob.
BOB	Fuck you. You see a little bird told me that you like me.
PATTY	Hey Bob, just think about all your other women.
BOB	What others? There's only Cathy. I mean we never talk when we're at work do we? You want to know something Patty . . . things aren't what they should be at home.
ANDY	How do you know, you're never there.
GAVIN	(*stirring*) Eh . . .
BOB	I love her . . . but . . . she doesn't really know me.
PATTY	Well don't you think you'd better go home then so she can get to know you?
BOB	We're not physical you know.
ANDY	Ha ha ha . . .
PATTY	No.
	(LEE *toots*.)
BOB	Not for months you know.
PATTY	Bob will you let me go please . . .
BOB	Look, I know you want to go . . . I do . . . but can we talk another time . . .
PATTY	Yeh, yeh of course we can.
BOB	Tomorrow . . .
PATTY	I've got to go Bob. Ok . . . ok. Ok darling. Look will you let me go Bob, I've really got to go. Really, please.
BOB	I photocopied my arse for you.
PATTY	I'm touched, I am — honest.
BOB	There's no one else.
PATTY	You're a lying sod.

BOB   I love my family Patty, I do. I love my kids. I love the little sods.

            (BOB *is now in tears*.)

PATTY   Is that why you're seeing other women Bob?

BOB   I'm not though, I'm not. Anyway we just talk. I don't actually do anything with her, you know. We just talk, I mean, I haven't been physical for years, do you know that? I have a pint, she has a vodka and tonic and we sit, we just sit, and talk. Just pass the time. I can't talk to Cathy, I mean I can't get through to her. Fucking hell, I wish I could get through to that woman. I love her . . . but . . . but . . . orrr.

ANDY   Take him home . . .

BOB   I do love her.

            (JO *enters*. LEE *toots*.)

PATTY   Hey come on Bob . . . come on. Come on, hey, it's supposed to be a party. (*She holds him*.)

BOB   (*crying*) Fucking hell, my life . . .

LEE   Glad I'm not married.

            (BOB *weeps*. PATTY *holds him*.)

BOB   Don't look at me.

PATTY   Come on . . . eh . . . come on.

BOB   Don't go Patty.

PATTY   I've got to Bob.

BOB   Stay here a bit . . . I'm all right, stay a bit.

PATTY   I can't . . .

JO   I thought he was driving you home?

ANDY   He is.

PATTY   Bob, Bob, I've really got to go, Bob. Look, let me go Bob, please. Please Bob, let me get up ok?

BOB	Don't.
PATTY	Bob, can you just let me go. Bob fuck off, all right?

(PATTY *pushes* BOB *onto the floor. He flails around trying to get to his feet while the others stifle their laughs.*)

BOB	(*sad*) Yeh, yeh, ok . . . ok. I've got the picture.
ANDY	Steady Bob. (*He loses his balance.*)
BOB	Do I get a kiss Pat? Just a kiss?
PATTY	I'll see you tomorrow.
BOB	Just a peck . . .

(PATTY *is about to depart. As she exits, she stands in some vomit that* PIPPA *has deposited upstage.*)

BOB	She needs a good man.
JO	Put a sock in it will you?
BOB	She needs a good man.
ANDY	Well you had your chance.
BOB	I need another drink.
ANDY	There is none.
BOB	Yes there is. I've got a bottle of brandy in my office. (*Exits.*) She needs a good man . . .

(PIPPA *enters.*)

PIPPA	Is there any mousse left?
LEE	Why will it be me anyway?
PIPPA	What are you prattling on about?
LEE	(*to* PIPPA) She said I was going to get the sack.
PIPPA	I did not. It might not be you anyway.

LEE	You think you know everything about this office don't you?
PIPPA	You said you weren't bothered anyway.
LEE	I'm not.
PIPPA	You are.
LEE	I'm not.
PIPPA	You are . . .
LEE	Look at Gavin, he's out of it. Hey, you should drink more often. Look at him, good party, eh?
ANDY	Brilliant.
LEE	(*going to* GAVIN) Don't sack me Gavin, I'm the only one who thinks you're a good bloke. (*Toots into* GAVIN'S *face*.) He's pissed up.
	(LEE *exits upstage.* PIPPA *continues to attempt to get* GAVIN *up on his feet.*)
PIPPA	Up, up . . . come on . . . let's see if you can do it. Good come on . . . Come on you silly man, get up. Get up . . . hey you. Not so bossy now are you? Hey, not so bossy now. Come on, get up. Let's make a night of it? Or are you too old? Ha ha, come on old man. Shall I take his trousers off?
	(*Silence.*)
	You know what? We could kill him, couldn't we?
ANDY	What?
PIPPA	If we wanted to we could kill him now.
ANDY	Eh?
PIPPA	We could throw him out of a window.
ANDY	Eh?
PIPPA	Yeh.
ANDY	Nooo.

PIPPA	Yeh, the three of us. Lift him up and throw him out.
ANDY	Yeh.
PIPPA	We could suffocate him.
ANDY	How . . .
PIPPA	Stuff paper down his mouth. Or set fire to him? Cover him in perfume and set him on fire.
ANDY	I haven't got a light.
PIPPA	I have. (*She produces a lighter.*)
JO	I thought you liked him?
PIPPA	We could do it couldn't we, if we wanted? I mean he does what he wants. Why can't we do what we want?
ANDY	We can't set him on fire.
PIPPA	Why?
ANDY	We haven't got enough perfume.
GAVIN	(*stirring*) Eh?
PIPPA	We're just thinking about setting fire to you Gavin, just hang on a minute.
GAVIN	Eh?
PIPPA	What about brandy?
ANDY	Bob's got some.
PIPPA	Brilliant, let's cover him in that.
ANDY	No.
PIPPA	Why?
ANDY	It'd be a waste of good brandy.
PIPPA	No it'd be brilliant that. Just drench him in it, light the blue touch paper and burn the bastard.
ANDY	It's a thought isn't it?

(GAVIN *begins to stir and move. He is in the angry state of drunkenness. Awkward, lucid, crazy, dangerous and absurd.*)

GAVIN   Off, get off. I'm here . . . don't worry, I'm here.

PIPPA   Do you want another drink?

GAVIN   Coffee.

PIPPA   There's no cups.

ANDY   Get him a brandy.

GAVIN   Ah . . . eh. Feels good. (*Sings.*) "I'm an alligator, I'm a mama papa coming for you." Bowie. ah, yes. Ziggy. "Ziggy played guitar. Jamming good with Weird and Gilly." Oh eh . . . brilliant album . . . "and the Spiders from Mars . . ."

PIPPA   Do you want to lay on the sofa? Shall I get him in the boardroom?

GAVIN   Jo and Andy, good man. Well in.

ANDY   Look at him, he's worth a fortune. And I bet he's in the bloody Masons.

PIPPA   The what?

ANDY   He's got a funny handshake. It's like a wet fish in your hand.

(GAVIN *has controlled himself and confronts* ANDY.)

GAVIN   I change what I want.

ANDY   Eh?

GAVIN   Your copy, puhhhh! I change it.

ANDY   I know that.

GAVIN   Don't ask me why I'm changing it. I change what I want, all right? And if you don't like it you know what you can do.

ANDY   I do.

GAVIN   Yeh?

ANDY   Yeh.

GAVIN   You're not a big man.

ANDY   I know that.

GAVIN   You are a nobody.

ANDY   That's right.

PIPPA   What's he on about?

GAVIN   There's people dying out there and what are you doing?
            Nothing. What am I doing, nothing, nothing, keeping
            my head down and getting on with it, frightened. Just
            getting on with our petty little lives frightened. There
            are people sleeping on the streets out there. Well fuck
            'em, that's what I say. But what do you say Andy? Save
            'em eh, save 'em, well use your money mate and go out
            and save 'em, go on. Can't you see it, if you're in this
            business, they can't exist. Or we're doomed.

ANDY   Are we?

GAVIN   We are now she's let us down. (*To* Jo. *A moment.*) Oh
            Caroline, Caroline, where the bloody hell is she?

PIPPA   Shall I get him to bed?

GAVIN   You know something?

ANDY   What?

GAVIN   You haven't threatened to leave this year. Why's that I
            wonder?

ANDY   I must be enjoying myself.

JO   Is he always like this?

ANDY   You should've seen him last year.

GAVIN   It's because you haven't got the guts.

PIPPA   Shall I get him a black coffee?

(GAVIN *grabs* PIPPA *and hugs her tight.*)

GAVIN   Oh eh . . . this is more like it.

PIPPA   What shall I do with him?

GAVIN   This more like it.

PIPPA   Shall I get you on the sofa, Gav?

GAVIN   Yeh. Get me on a sofa.

PIPPA   Are you all right?

GAVIN   Yeh.

PIPPA   I'll take him in the boardroom and put him on the
             whatsit.

JO   I think we should've killed him.

PIPPA   I'll just loosen his clothes, shall I?

             (PIPPA *manages to get* GAVIN *off stage.* GAVIN *is
             comatose as he leaves the stage.* JO *and* ANDY *look at
             each other. Silence.*)

ANDY   It's been a good night hasn't it?

JO   Has it?

ANDY   Well nobody's died. I thought you weren't coming?

JO   Yeh well.

ANDY   Another drink?

JO   Why not?

             (ANDY *stands. He looks for a bottle of wine, but can
             only find a half full can of lager which he pours some
             into a wine glass for* JO. *He has the other half of the
             lager himself. He sits in the swivel chair and propels
             himself downstage in it by using his legs.*)

ANDY   He told me about Patterson.

JO   Oh leave it.

ANDY	What a shit.
JO	I half expected it.
ANDY	Really?
JO	You can see what he's like a mile off.
ANDY	He wants to support you.
JO	Does he?
ANDY	So he says.
JO	So what's he going to do?
ANDY	I don't know.
JO	Maybe Pat should go and see him next time.
ANDY	Or Pippa?
JO	She'd frighten him to death.

(ANDY *and* JO *laugh and we can see they are quite bonded. Silence.*)

ANDY	I'm sorry Jo. If I've been a bit . . .
JO	What?
ANDY	Well you know . . .
JO	What?
ANDY	. . . slow.
JO	Slow?
ANDY	Yeh.
JO	At what?
ANDY	Responding.
JO	Oh right.
ANDY	I haven't done it for ages.
JO	No?

ANDY	I mean it's difficult.
JO	Is it?
ANDY	Oh Jo!
JO	What?
ANDY	Oh!
JO	What?
ANDY	Oh Jo?
JO	What're you on about?
ANDY	Oh, Jo Stewart!
JO	Andy?
ANDY	And I love Jen, you know.
JO	Yeh?
ANDY	I do.
JO	I know.
ANDY	And the bloody kids, God bless 'em.
JO	Of course you do.
ANDY	And up here. (*His head.*) I can manage it. I mean in my head Jo, I'm a Chippendale.
JO	Really?
ANDY	This is very dangerous, don't you think?
JO	Well. . .
ANDY	Very dangerous.
JO	Well it could be.
ANDY	Oh dear Jo.
JO	What?
ANDY	Well, us.
JO	What about us?

ANDY   I do like you, you know.

JO   I like you.

ANDY   I know.

JO   I mean . . .

ANDY   Oh hell.

JO   What's wrong?

ANDY   Don't tease me.

JO   I'm not.

ANDY   You've been doing that for the last five months.

JO   What?

ANDY   Teasing me.

JO   No way.

ANDY   You have. You might not know it but you have. Oh
            what? All the little chats we've had. All the intimate
            details. Your hands all over me in the pub, knees
            touching over dinner. Oh Jo!

JO   Andy?

ANDY   Don't tell me you haven't. Don't tell me I've been
            fantasising about nothing. Every time you smiled at me,
            or touched me, or got close I've been jotting it down on
            my score sheet. Jo, for the last five months I've been
            analyzing your every bodily movement. Don't tell me
            I've been basing all this on a fucking nervous twitch.
            Because I will die.

JO   I do like you.

ANDY   Do you?

JO   This is stupid. We're two grown up people.

ANDY   I know.

JO   What can I say?

ANDY	Dunno.
JO	You're a lovely man.
ANDY	Am I?
JO	Yeh.
ANDY	Oh dear.
JO	And I haven't been teasing you, you know, really.
ANDY	It's all in my head Jo.
JO	I know.
ANDY	I mean what about Neil?
JO	What about Jenny?
ANDY	Oh Jo.
JO	Me and Neil have been at breaking point.
ANDY	Oh God.
JO	He's probably all over one of the secretaries . . .
ANDY	Oh Jo.
JO	You grow away . . .
ANDY	I know . . .
JO	It's Christmas.
ANDY	I know.
JO	What are we saying?
ANDY	I dunno.
JO	This is insane, isn't it?
ANDY	I know.
JO	You're a lovely sensitive man.
ANDY	I didn't think you liked me . . .
JO	Oh Andy . . .

ANDY   I'm a fart.

JO   You're not.

ANDY   Neil's probably a rugby player or . . .

JO   You're just different.

ANDY   Oh Jo. Gorr, I think . . . I mean. I really think you are,
          you know?

JO   Yeh.

ANDY   I just don't think I'd be able to live up to expectations.

JO   I don't have any.

ANDY   I mean it is Christmas, isn't it?

JO   It is.

ANDY   Yeh.

JO   Yeh.

          (*A beat.*)

          Why don't you kiss me then?

          (*A beat.*)

ANDY   What?

JO   I said, I why don't you kiss me?

ANDY   Bloody hell.

JO   Yeh.

ANDY   Why am I shaking? Gorr Jo, why am I lying to myself
          all the time?

JO   Why don't you just get on with it?

ANDY   Because I'm nervous.

JO   So am I.

ANDY   My lips are trembling.

JO   Just kiss me.

ANDY   My whole face is tingling.

JO   Is it?

ANDY   No tongues.

JO   No.

ANDY   Just a Christmas kiss?

JO   Yeh.

(ANDY *has made his way over to* JO. *He is being held back by some strange inability. When he eventually kisses* JO *it is gentle to begin with but then it becomes more passionate. They stop and pull away.*)

ANDY   Merry Christmas.

JO   Merry Christmas.

(*They kiss again even more passionately.* ANDY *pulls himself from her.*)

ANDY   Oh God.

JO   Merry merry Christmas . . .

(ANDY *grabs her and they kiss even more passionately. Each of them begins to fondle the other's body, it is wild and mad. Suddenly* ANDY *stops and steps back from her. They are both dying to take it further, but neither of them dare.*)

ANDY   Hang on . . .

JO   What?

ANDY   Shit . . .

JO   What . . .

ANDY   Shit.

JO   Is it no good?

ANDY	No good? It's excellent.
Jo	What's wrong?
ANDY	Wait a minute.
Jo	What for?
ANDY	Oh sorry. Shit.
Jo	Sorry?
ANDY	It's not you, it's not you.
Jo	Come on . . .
ANDY	It's me Jo. It's my fault it's my problem. Oh shit, my heart's going.
Jo	Are you ok?
ANDY	I think I'm going to have a panic do.
Jo	Don't die on me.
ANDY	My legs are shaking.
Jo	Mine are.
ANDY	That's all I can manage.
Jo	Story of my life.
ANDY	I'm sorry.
Jo	Oh what am I doing? This is stupid.
ANDY	It's not you.
Jo	Well who the hell is it then? What am I doing here, I must be insane.
ANDY	Jo honestly, sorry.
Jo	Sorry?
ANDY	You're great. I mean oh yes. Oh yes.
Jo	Oh thanks.

ANDY	You're wonderful, you know, very lippy.
Jo	What?
ANDY	Very sucky, you know very . . . (*Slurps.*) Very, oh yes.
Jo	Yeh?
ANDY	Very slurpy nice . . .
Jo	Thank you for that. God, I must be mad.
ANDY	It's me, I'm the problem.
Jo	No, it's me, I've always been lousy at kissing. But I didn't think I was so bad.
ANDY	It's not you.
Jo	It is I know.
ANDY	No.
Jo	This is ridiculous.
ANDY	I know that.
Jo	What's wrong with you?

(Jo *sidles away from* ANDY, *their lust has to be quelled.*)

ANDY	Just stand over there away from me.
Jo	What's the matter with you?

(Jo *and* ANDY *stand apart from each other. They still want to be close but sense and sensibility is prevailing.*)

ANDY	Shit my legs are still going. Hey listen, I was in bed with you, married and we'd got three kids. That's what's the matter.
Jo	Let's leave it then.
ANDY	Yeh, let's.
Jo	Just forget it. Forget it. Don't talk about it. I just want you to know that I have never done that before. I have never been like that before. And I'm sorry.

ANDY   It was me Jo, it was me. I'm all over the place. My legs
                are still . . .

                (LEE, *bedraggled and sad, enters from upstage. He is
                more sober now, but still slightly at odds with the world.*
                ANDY *is trying to get his legs from shaking.*)

LEE   Arrggh, what are you two up to then? I knew you two
                would be up to something. I can tell a mile off.

JO   We're just talking.

LEE   Oh aye?

JO   Why?

LEE   What's wrong with your leg?

ANDY   Just lost a bit of . . .

LEE   Arrggh . . .

ANDY   What?

LEE   Arrggh . . .

ANDY   I thought you were going to another party?

LEE   No. I've been drinking coffee from the machine. I've
                burnt my lips and all, couldn't get my mouth under.

                (LEE *demonstrates that he has been trying to put his
                mouth under the cups socket in the coffee machine.*)

JO   Well it's big enough.

LEE   There's been hell on in town, did you hear the sirens?
                I could see something going on. I was just stood there
                like Good King Wenslessless-less . . . last.

ANDY   Right.

LEE   So has Pippa gone?

JO   Yeh.

LEE	Oh well, better luck next time. I don't think she likes me anyway but I could've walked her home.
ANDY	Why, what's happened to your car?
LEE	Battery's flat. Ridiculous isn't it? I'm brilliant with computers and I've left my bloody car lights on.
JO	Anyway. I think I'd better . . .
ANDY	You going?
JO	I think I'd better.
ANDY	Yeh, Yeh. Will you be . . . ?
JO	Yeh. I'd better. I think.
LEE	Hey Jo, any chance of a Christmas kiss then?
JO	I thought you'd burnt your lips?
LEE	I have but . . .
JO	Maybe next year.
ANDY	Yeh yeh, maybe next year Lee, all right?
LEE	Shit rolls downwards, right.
ANDY	Right.
JO	See you then.
ANDY	Yeh. Right.
	(JO *reluctantly exits.* ANDY *stands around. He cannot watch her leave.* LEE *sits.* ANDY *is confused.*)
LEE	Sorry?
ANDY	What?
LEE	You and her?
ANDY	Oh, it, erm . . .
LEE	Sorry.
ANDY	Just having a chat.

LEE   Sorry I didn't . . .

ANDY   No.

LEE   Bad timing, eh?

ANDY   I thought you'd gone.

LEE   Arrggh.

ANDY   Anyway.

LEE   Where's Bob?

ANDY   I think he, erm . . .

LEE   Did he pull?

ANDY   No, sadly. Another year without any success.

LEE   Good old Bob.

ANDY   Anyway. I think that's about it for me.

LEE   I thought Bob was driving you back?

ANDY   He was, but . . .

LEE   Better get off then.

ANDY   I'll walk into town, I think.

LEE   It's snowing.

ANDY   I need a bit of fresh air. In fact I need a lot of fresh air.
         The walk'll sober me up.

LEE   Jo will have gone.

ANDY   With any luck.

LEE   Arrggh.

ANDY   Anyway. Back to reality.

LEE   That's right.

ANDY   Take care.

LEE   Merry Christmas.

ANDY	And you mate, and if Bob materializes tell him I've . . .
LEE	Oh yeh don't worry, I'll tell him.

(ANDY *departs from the office. Grabs a coat and leaves.* LEE *is sat alone on stage. Silence.* BOB *enters. He has drunk a half bottle of brandy, and he has a long fax which he places on a desk. This is a fax of women's bottoms which has come from Patterson's.* BOB *reclines like a king.*)

BOB	Brandy. At long last. A night cap?
LEE	Just one.
BOB	All gone?
LEE	Just me and you.
BOB	This is more like it. Nice and quiet. It's usually just me left at the end. I stayed till the next day once. Or was it the day after? What are you grinning at?
LEE	Oh dear.
BOB	What?
LEE	Oh dear me.
BOB	What, what?
LEE	I've just caught 'em at it.
BOB	Who?
LEE	Jo and Andy.
BOB	What?
LEE	On the table.
BOB	What??
LEE	Just finishing off, when I came in. Legs trembling, shirt out, sweating like a dog — must have been a real bone-shaker.
BOB	You're joking?

LEE	He must have had her on the desk. Oh yes.
BOB	Oh yes.
LEE	They were just getting their gear back on when I came in.
BOB	What?
LEE	Yeh, both of 'em were stripped down. Flesh all over the place. Oh man. Yeh.
BOB	I wouldn't mind some of that.
LEE	Oh yes please.
BOB	Oh yes.
LEE	They were very . . . when I came in.
BOB	Oh yes.
LEE	You could cut the atmosphere. Suddenly she's off, he hangs about and then . . . legs it. Walking home.
BOB	Guilt.
LEE	Walk home in the snow. Like that good King Wenslessless-thing.
BOB	Yeh?
LEE	Oh yes, they must have been having a right go.
BOB	Oh good man. Good man. What a sly . . . oh yes, brilliant, ha ha. Oh what a sly little pinko bastard. I knew it. I knew it . . .

(LEE *has wandered over to the faxes and he begins to peruse them.*)

LEE	Oh yes.
BOB	I knew it. Thank God somebody actually did it.

(LEE *picks up the elongated fax.*)

| LEE | What's all this? |

Bob	Oh yeh, some more bums from Patterson's.
Lee	And we thought their party was boring!
Bob	That's right.
Lee	These are all women's.
Bob	It's their typing pool, by the looks of it.
Lee	What sort of a party are they having if they're getting up to all that?
Bob	A very good party.
Lee	Yeh.
Bob	A very very good party.
Lee	It looks like they've been hit by the recession. There's one here with no knickers on.
Bob	I think you'll find that's a man.
Lee	It must be the light.
Bob	I double-checked.
Lee	(*looking at the fax*) There's one here must be well over fifty.
Bob	We never learn do we?
Lee	No.
Bob	Never learn.
Lee	Are you going home then?
Bob	Dunno.
Lee	Won't she expect you?
Bob	Dunno.
Lee	(*still looking at the fax*) Must be well over fifty, that one.
Bob	It's a bloody mess, isn't it?

LEE   I think I'm in the wrong job.

BOB   Yeh.

LEE   Yeh.

BOB   Not only are we in the wrong job Lee, it looks like
             we've been at the wrong fucking party.

             (BOB *begins to laugh, the laugh becomes a cackle.*
             Music plays and the lights fade.)

                          Scene Three

The next morning. Debris everywhere. It is early. We see the cold light
of day on the office. GAVIN emerges from his office. He is absolutely
the worse for wear. He grunts and surveys the mess.

GAVIN   Never again.

             (*He looks around at the mess. He pays particular*
             interest to the fax of bottoms from Patterson's.)

             Oh Bob!

             (*Slowly, sheepishly PIPPA enters. She is still wearing*
             her party dress, her hair is all over the place and she
             carries her shoes.)

PIPPA   Morning.

GAVIN   Huh?

PIPPA   Morning.

GAVIN   Is it?

PIPPA   Shall I make some coffee?

GAVIN   Would you?

PIPPA   Black?

GAVIN   Very.

PIPPA   Right.

GAVIN	And then clean some of this mess up, will you?
PIPPA	Me?
GAVIN	Just make a start, will you?
PIPPA	Yeh.
GAVIN	Look at it.
PIPPA	I feel a bit rough.
GAVIN	Mmmmm.
PIPPA	Do you?
GAVIN	Yeh. Yeh.
PIPPA	Did you sleep all right?
GAVIN	Er, yeh. I did yeh.
PIPPA	Good.
GAVIN	Yeh, yeh not bad.
PIPPA	A bit cramped but . . .
GAVIN	Yeh.
PIPPA	Warm though, better than my flat.
GAVIN	Yeh, coffee?
PIPPA	Want some?
GAVIN	Better go and get some plastic cups.
	(*A beat.*)
PIPPA	It was all right, wasn't it?
GAVIN	What?
PIPPA	Last night.
GAVIN	Oh that . . .
PIPPA	All right, eh?
GAVIN	(*avoiding*) Yeh, yeh.

PIPPA	All right, eh?
GAVIN	Of course.
PIPPA	I've got a stiff neck.
GAVIN	Eh?
PIPPA	A stiff neck . . .
GAVIN	Yeh, yeh I have.
PIPPA	Can you remember?
GAVIN	Eh?
PIPPA	Can you remember what you said?
GAVIN	Eh?
PIPPA	Last night?
GAVIN	What?
PIPPA	You said some really funny things.
GAVIN	I bet I did.
PIPPA	You were coming out with all sorts.
GAVIN	Really?
PIPPA	What did you call me?
GAVIN	Yeh ok, spare me the detail.
PIPPA	Rubber bunny, wasn't it?
GAVIN	Coffee?
PIPPA	Oh yeh.

(PIPPA *makes her way towards the coffee machine exit.*)

GAVIN	Erm, Pip?
PIPPA	Yeh?
GAVIN	Don't you know?

PIPPA	What?
GAVIN	You know . . .
PIPPA	Oh no, right. Not a word.
GAVIN	Right.
PIPPA	Well we hardly did anything, did we?
GAVIN	That's right, we hardly did anything . . .
PIPPA	I mean you couldn't.
GAVIN	Yeh, yeh, that's right.
PIPPA	Funny that, wasn't it?
GAVIN	Yeh.
PIPPA	So when's the next party? I can't wait.
	(PATTY *enters, catching the tail end of these lines. She is clearly shaken by* PIPPA *still in her party wear.*)
PATTY	Morning.
PIPPA	Morning.
PATTY	There's a funny smell in here.
PIPPA	I think Bob must have died.
PATTY	I suppose somebody ought to sort out all this lot.
PIPPA	We were just going to . . .
PATTY	That's all right, I can make a start.
GAVIN	We'll get somebody in. It's no problem.
PIPPA	I'll go and put the coffee on, shall I?
	(PIPPA *exits,* GAVIN *watches her go, and the horror of what he appears to have done becomes palpable to him. Silence between him and* PATTY.)
PATTY	Good night?
GAVIN	Yeh.

PATTY	Good.
GAVIN	That's right.
PATTY	We might need to talk about the regatta account before the New Year.
GAVIN	Yes, right.
PATTY	When you've got the time . . .
GAVIN	This was just . . .
PATTY	It's none of my business, Gavin.
GAVIN	No, right.
PATTY	Yeh.

(PATTY *disappears. As she does* BOB *enters from another entrance. He is still wearing a party hat and is covered in streamers. He has clearly slept in the office.*)

BOB	I should go home. My mouth tastes like bird shit.
GAVIN	Thanks for that.
BOB	Oh God . . .
GAVIN	Didn't make it home then?
BOB	Couldn't.
GAVIN	No.
BOB	I slept in Market Research. Ingrid had already gone, worse luck.
GAVIN	Oh Bob?
BOB	Great night.
GAVIN	So I gather.

(LEE *enters. He is bright and breezy, clearly happy.*)

LEE	(*seeing* BOB) Oh yes, still wanting to keep the party going Bob, that takes courage.

BOB   I feel like shit.

LEE   You look like a zombie.

BOB   I feel like one.

LEE   Oh man, what a night.

GAVIN   At least he enjoyed it . . .

LEE   Oh look at it. (*The office.*)

BOB   I think I've died and gone to heaven.

LEE   Weird night wasn't it?

GAVIN   Oh dear . . .

LEE   I'm walking home right, about half three, and I see this girl I was at college with. Haven't seen her since we left. She works over in Booths, so I thought, "hello". The next thing you know, we're snogging and I'm staying at hers. I didn't even try, I couldn't believe it. I'd spent six hours wasting time here, I walk out onto the streets and meet an angel. Weird, eh?

BOB   I can't bear this, this is part of a conspiracy, see.

           (BOB *hobbles carefully out of the office.*)

LEE   Yeh she just came out of Clough Road, and bang. Great stuff. And I'm seeing her again tonight.

GAVIN   You lucky sod.

LEE   Great, isn't it?

           (PIPPA *enters.*)

PIPPA   Gavin, telephone.

LEE   Oh right, another dirty stop out. What have you been up to, not been shagging Bob have you?

PIPPA   No.

LEE   Oh yeh, who've you been shagging then?

GAVIN	Who is it?
PIPPA	Mr Patterson, it's on your office line.
GAVIN	Great. Just what I need! You're a lucky sod, Nero.

(GAVIN *exits.* PIPPA *feels embarrassed as the contrast of her stood in a mini skirt and* LEE *wrapped for snow sinks in. Silence.*)

PIPPA	Is it cold out?
LEE	It would be dressed like that.
PIPPA	Yeh I . . .
LEE	Arrggh!
PIPPA	Oh don't, I feel awful.
LEE	You and . . . ?
PIPPA	Don't.
LEE	Oh no . . . I can't stand it.
PIPPA	Yeh well . . .
LEE	That's awful, I mean . . . oh no . . . oh brilliant.
PIPPA	Nothing happened.
LEE	Oh yeh?
PIPPA	No, honest.
LEE	Get off, we all know what Gavin's like.
PIPPA	No honest, listen . . .
LEE	Get off.
PIPPA	No listen, honest, I wish something had, but he was useless, all mouth. Honest.
LEE	He's past it, man.

(*A phone rings in the office. It is under some debris.* PIPPA *looks for the phone, and manages to extract the receiver from between wine bottles and streamers.*)

PIPPA	Good morning, the Chapman and Howard, oh look at this! (*She has mousse on the phone and her hands.*) Sorry. Hello. Shit. No, he's not here at the moment. Can I take a message? Ok, hang on. No we had a party, yeh it's chaos, yeh everybody's naked. Three people died.
LEE	Four.
PIPPA	Might be more apparently.
LEE	The ambulance has just arrived.
PIPPA	The ambulance has just arrived. No it's a joke . . . Yeh . . . hang on, pen. Pen. Right. I've got that. To ring urgently, I've got that. Bye. Thank you for calling . . . Gone.
LEE	Who was it?
	(LEE *and* PIPPA *are laughing.* GAVIN *enters from the gantry. He is furious.*)
GAVIN	Can we get something done, or are you two going to sit there like dummies all morning? I'm working my heart out here and you two are pissing about all the time. And I want a word with you sunshine.
LEE	Me?
GAVIN	And can we get somebody to come and clear up all this mess for the hundredth time, or do you want me to come and start to do the whole lot myself? I thought I said to contract some new cleaners? Can you remember that darling or are you completely fucking useless?
	(GAVIN *exits from the gantry.* PIPPA *is very upset by this onslaught, she cries.* PIPPA *exits,* LEE *begins to look busy.* ANDY *enters.*)
ANDY	Morning.
LEE	Is it?
ANDY	What's all the shouting?
LEE	He's on the war path.

ANDY   The party's over then, is it?

                (LEE *exits.* ANDY *looks at the mess. He begins to clear*
                his desk. He looks at the note that PIPPA *has left on her*
                desk. He picks up the note and puts it in his pocket.
                PATTY *enters, and makes her way across stage. She*
                passes ANDY *almost without recognition.*)

PATTY   Patterson looks like he's pulling the campaign.

ANDY   Oh wonderful.

                (PATTY *exits.* ANDY *sits and thinks.* BOB, *feeling a little*
                better, enters. He sees ANDY *and is full of glee.*)

BOB   Oh yes, here he is.

ANDY   Morning.

BOB   Bloody hell, you're a sly one.

ANDY   Not this morning, Bob.

BOB   Oh yes . . .

ANDY   Please.

BOB   I mean, I thought I was a pig sniffing after Ingrid, but
                you take the biscuit.

ANDY   What are you on about?

BOB   Banging her one in here . . .

ANDY   You what?

BOB   Oh yes . . .

ANDY   Hey listen . . .

BOB   I didn't think you had it in you.

ANDY   Pack it in.

BOB   Which table was it?

ANDY   Pack it in Bob.

BOB   Dirty sod.

ANDY	Listen . . .
BOB	I think it's brilliant!
ANDY	Stop it . . .
BOB	I bet she didn't say that . . .
ANDY	I'm warning you.
BOB	Done something naughty, have you?
ANDY	I'm telling you to pack it in.
BOB	Oh yeh?
ANDY	I mean it.
BOB	What's Jenny going to say to that then?
ANDY	Just shut it . . .
BOB	Oh very nice.

(ANDY *stands. He is now furious and we haven't seen him like this before. He walks towards* BOB.)

ANDY	Listen just pack it fucking in Bob, now I'm warning you!
BOB	Are you?

(ANDY *is very, very angry.*)

ANDY	I mean it! I mean it! I mean it! Get off my back, you sad bastard. Get off my back and get your own life sorted out man, Jesus, you're killing that woman, she's on the phone to Jenny every fucking night in tears.
BOB	What's that got to do with you?
ANDY	Just get off my back.
BOB	You're in a mess.
ANDY	Am I?
BOB	Did you do her or what? Let's hear the truth.

ANDY	Why, is that what you'd have done?
BOB	Yes I would.
ANDY	Oh great!
BOB	I'm not dead.
ANDY	Oh no?
BOB	I know I'm trapped.
ANDY	Oh yeh?
BOB	But I'm not dead.
ANDY	Aren't you?
BOB	Which is more than I can say for you.
ANDY	Well you don't look it.
BOB	I make sure I'm alive two days a month.
ANDY	I know, I've heard.
BOB	When I go away I make sure I have a good time.
ANDY	Good for you.
BOB	That's why Gav never sends you into Europe — you wouldn't know what to do with yourself.
ANDY	Is that right?
BOB	So you didn't bang her one then?
ANDY	No, no I didn't.
BOB	I knew it.
ANDY	So there you go, sorry Bob, but we're not all pigs.
BOB	But you want to don't you?
ANDY	You're not worth it.
BOB	Admit it.
ANDY	Jesus.

BOB	Go on.
ANDY	Pack it in.
BOB	Go on.
ANDY	You're a . . .
BOB	Admit it, admit it. Admit it!
ANDY	(*shouting*) All right, all right. I admit it. I admit it. God, I can't get the woman out of my head. I'm obsessed by her, I think she's gorgeous, christ almighty, it's driving me fucking crazy. I'm in love with the poor woman, but what can I do, what can I do? It's eating at me, it's killing me, it's killing me and Jenny, Christ what can I do? Yes I admit it, I think she is wonderful!
BOB	See?
ANDY	Yeh.
BOB	See?
ANDY	All right!
BOB	I knew.

(BOB *turns to leave the office.* ANDY *sits. He is quite upset. He is shaking. He looks at the note from his pocket, which he took from* PIPPA'S *desk. As he sits* JO *enters. She looks splendid. They are very awkward with each other.*)

JO	Morning.
ANDY	Morning.
JO	All right?
ANDY	Yeh.
JO	Erm, good last night, wasn't it?
ANDY	Yeh.
JO	Yeh.

ANDY   Brilliant.

JO   Yeh.

ANDY   Back to reality.

JO   Yeh.

ANDY   Anyway?

JO   Mess in here.

ANDY   Yeh.

JO   Anyway . . .

                (JO *makes to exit.*)

ANDY   Oh Jo, if you see Bob, tell him Cathy called, will you?
                It's urgent apparently, she wants him to give her a call.

JO   Yeh, yeh I will.

ANDY   Good.

JO   Which Cathy is it?

ANDY   Could be either.

JO   Oh, right.

ANDY   Yeh.

JO   Oops?

ANDY   Oops, yeh.

JO   Poor old Bob.

                (JO *has exited.* ANDY *sits at his desk. He sees the hooter
                which* LEE *had earlier. He slowly plays with it.*)

ANDY   Yeh, poor old Bob!

                (ANDY *makes a clownish noise with the hooter. He sits
                with it in his mouth, then begins to cry. Lights fade.
                Silence. Playout music —"It's Raining Men" by the
                Weather Girls. Curtain.*)